Pocket
BERLIN

TOP SIGHTS · LOCAL LIFE · MADE EASY

Andrea Schulte-Peevers

In This Book

QuickStart Guide

Your keys to understanding the city – we help you decide what to do and how to do it

Need to Know
Tips for a smooth trip

Neighbourhoods
What's where

Explore Berlin

The best things to see and do, neighbourhood by neighbourhood

Top Sights
Make the most of your visit

Local Life
The insider's city

The Best of Berlin

The city's highlights in handy lists to help you plan

Best Walks
See the city on foot

Berlin's Best...
The best experiences

Survival Guide

Tips and tricks for a seamless, hassle-free city experience

Getting Around
Travel like a local

Essential Information
Including where to stay

Our selection of the city's best places to eat, drink and experience:

◉ **Sights**

✖ **Eating**

🚻 **Drinking**

✿ **Entertainment**

🔒 **Shopping**

These symbols give you the vital information for each listing:

📞 Telephone Numbers	👪 Family-Friendly
⊙ Opening Hours	🐾 Pet-Friendly
🅿 Parking	🚌 Bus
⊝ Nonsmoking	🚢 Ferry
@ Internet Access	🚊 Tram
🛜 Wi-Fi Access	🚆 Train
🌱 Vegetarian Selection	
📖 English-Language Menu	

Find each listing quickly on maps for each neighbourhood:

Bar Hemingway

16 🚻 Map p233, B2

Legend has it that Hemi self, wielding a machine ...rate this timber-pan ...tered bar during ... showpiece is a ...en by Papa an ...s.com; Hôtel Rit ⊙6.30pm-2a

6 ◉ Plac ...

QuickStart Guide

Welcome to Berlin

Berlin is a bon vivant, passionately feasting on the smorgasbord of life. A contagious energy permeates its cafes, bars, clubs and classic cabarets. Indie boutiques and progressive restaurants compete for your time with world-class museums and striking landmarks that reflect the city's riveting history. Must-sees or aimless explorations Berlin delivers it all in one exciting and memorable package.

The glass-domed Reichstag building (p24)
THOMAS WINZ/LONELY PLANET IMAGES ©

Berlin
Top Sights

Reichstag & Government Quarter (p24)

Views are mesmerising from the dazzling glass cupola atop the Reichstag, the seat of the German parliament and the stately focal point of the reunited country's government quarter.

Brandenburg Gate & Pariser Platz (p26)

Prussian emperors, Napoleon and Hitler have marched through this neoclassical royal city gate, once trapped east of the Berlin Wall and now a symbol of reunited Germany.

PAOLO CORDELLI/LONELY PLANET IMAGES ©

Holocaust Memorial (p28)

Peter Eisenman poignantly captures the horror of the Nazi-inflicted Jewish mass murder with this vast undulating maze of tomblike concrete plinths.

Pergamonmuseum (p42)

Walk in the footsteps of Greeks, Romans and other ancient societies, whose monumental architecture, showcased in this museum, attests to their astonishingly high levels of civilisation.

PAOLO CORDELLI/LONELY PLANET IMAGES ©

IAIN MASTERTON/ALAMY ©

Neues Museum (p46)

Egyptian Queen Nefertiti is the most famous resident at this top-ranked museum, beautifully reconstructed by David Chipperfield and also sheltering a feast of findings going back to prehistoric times.

Gemäldegalerie (p56)

Rembrandt is here, Caravaggio too. Botticelli, Rubens, Vermeer – need we say more? Your spirits will soar as you gaze upon centuries worth of masterpieces by Europe's art-world stars.

Potsdamer Platz
(p60)

A post-reunification re-interpretation of Berlin's one-time equivalent of Times Square, the city's newest quarter shows off the talents of seminal architects of our times, including Renzo Piano and Helmut Jahn.

Jüdisches Museum
(p68)

The 2000-year-old tale of Jews in Germany is a fascinating one, but just as powerful is the heart-wrenching metaphorical language of Daniel Libeskind's extraordinary zinc-clad museum building.

Gedenkstätte Berliner Mauer (p74)

It's rather ironic that Berlin's biggest tourist attraction no longer exists. To get under the skin of the Berlin Wall mystery, build a visit of this indoor-outdoor memorial into your schedule.

East Side Gallery
(p102)

On the longest surviving stretch of the Berlin Wall, more than a hundred international artists have translated their feelings about the barrier's collapse into powerful murals.

Schloss Charlottenburg
(p134)

Prussian royals sure knew how to live it up, as you'll discover on a tour of the fancifully decorated living quarters of this grand palace attached to lushly landscaped gardens.

Schloss & Park Sanssouci (p138)

It's practically impossible not to be enchanted by this rambling palace ensemble dreamed up by King Frederick the Great, and merely a short train ride away in Potsdam.

Berlin Local Life

Insider tips to help you find the real city

After checking out Berlin's top sights, here's how you can experience what makes the city tick. Eclectic shopping strips, charismatic residential areas, chameleonesque neighbourhoods, neuron-destroying party quarters and even a 'boring-Sunday-antidote' are all features that make up the Berliner's Berlin.

An Afternoon in the Bergmannkiez (p70)

▶ Food market
▶ Eclectic shopping

Bisecting Kreuzberg's quieter and more bourgeois western section, Bergmannstrasse is a vibrant and colourful strip teeming with fun cafes, indie boutiques and speciality stores anchored by a fabulous food hall. Relax on the leafy hill that gave Kreuzberg its name, then contemplate the resilience of the human spirit at the Berlin Airlift Memorial.

Nosing Around Neukölln (p98)

▶ Vibrant food market
▶ Relaxed bar-hopping

Berlin's newest 'it' quarter is a shape-shifter, a dynamic and restless animal fed by an appetite for diversity and creativity. An exploration here is bound to be an eye-opener, perhaps even a glimpse into future trends. We can only provide suggestions on where to start, but give in to the local DIY spirit and you'll soon make your own discoveries.

Sundays Around the Mauerpark (p112)

▶ Fabulous flea market
▶ Coffee culture

When it comes to the Mauerpark, we have to agree with the tens of thousands of locals and visitors: there are few, if any, better places to be on a Sunday, especially a sunny one. A fabulous flea market, killer outdoor karaoke, barbecues and bands, all in a place once bifurcated by the Berlin Wall – what more could you wish for?

Exploring Many-Sided Schöneberg (p132)

▶ Farmers market
▶ Boutique shopping

Often overshadowed by Kurfürstendamm to the west and Kreuzberg to the east, Schöneberg deserves the spotlight in its own right. It's a largely residential but engagingly eclectic neighbourhood where greying suits rub shoulders with party-

Grocery store on Bergmanstrasse, Kreuzberg

Handbags, Mauerpark flea market

DAVID PEEVERS/LONELY PLANET IMAGES ©

hearty gays, ex-hippies and Turkish immigrants. Plenty of street cafes provide perfect people-watching perches.

Kotti Bar-Hop (p88)

▶ Bars for all persuasions
▶ Restorative fast-food joints

It takes a nanosecond to figure out that Berlin has no shortage of libation stations. By our estimation, the vibrantly gritty area around Kottbusser Tor U-Bahn station has some of the city's best, and all conveniently within stumbling distance of each other. No matter whether you're the beer or cocktail type, you'll find a favourite booze burrow here.

Other great places to experience the city like a local:

Rosenthaler Platz: Snack Central (p82)

Trendy Torstrasse (p84)

All Aboard the Badeschiff (p97)

Dreamy Ice Cream (p108)

Knaackstrasse Cafe Scene (p116)

Berlin's 'Little Asia' (p129)

Ku'damm: Shop 'til You Drop (p131)

Berlin
Day Planner

Day One

One day in Berlin? Follow this whirlwind itinerary to earn bragging rights for having seen all the key sights. Book ahead for an early lift ride up to the dome of the **Reichstag** (p24), then snap a picture of the **Brandenburg Gate** (p26) before exploring the maze of the **Holocaust Memorial** (p28) and admiring the contemporary architecture of **Potsdamer Platz** (p60). Ponder Nazi horrors at the **Topographie des Terrors** (p63) and Cold War madness at **Checkpoint Charlie** (p63).

Pop into the **Friedrichstadt-passagen** (p39) for a dose of retail therapy before a late lunch at **Augustiner am Gendarmenmarkt** (p36). Pick up a chocolate treat at **Fassbender & Rausch** (p39), then make your way to Museum Island via **Gendarmenmarkt** (p32). Spend at least an hour marvelling at the antique treasures at the **Pergamonmuseum** (p42), then take a leisurely meander around the Scheunenviertel, perhaps scheduling a coffee break at **Barcomi's Deli** (p82).

Come dinnertime, report to **Hart-weizen** (p80) for superb Italian or **Chén Chè** (p80) for Vietnamese, and wrap up the day with drinks at the **Neue Odessa Bar** (p83).

Day Two

Kick off day two coming to grips with what life in Berlin was like when the Wall still stood at the **Gedenkstätte Berliner Mauer** (p74). To intensify the experience, head to Warschauer Strasse U-/S-Bahn station and study the colourful murals decorating the **East Side Gallery** (p102), a 1.3km-long stretch of original Wall.

For lunch, train it back to Alexander-platz and either go hearty at **Zur Letzten Instanz** (p52) or healthy at **Dolores** (p81). Launch the afternoon's sightseeing with peeking into daily life east of the Iron Curtain at the **DDR Museum** (p49), then digest your impressions on a one-hour **river cruise** (p50) around Museum Island. Afterwards, report for your audience with Queen Nefertiti at the stunningly reconstructed **Neues Museum** (p46) and perhaps pop into the nearby **Humboldt-Box** (p49) to learn about the reconstruction of the Prussian royal city palace taking shape right here.

Relax over a memorable meat-free meal at **Cookies Cream** (p36) or travel back to the Golden Twenties at the cosy **Chamäleon Varieté** (p84).

Short on time?

We've arranged Berlin's must-sees into these day-by-day itineraries to make sure you see the very best of the city in the time you have available.

Day Three

☼ Day three starts at **Schloss Charlottenburg** (p134), where you shouldn't miss the Neuer Flügel (New Wing) or a spin around the lovely gardens. Take the U2 from Sophie-Charlotte-Platz to Zoologischer Garten, meditate on the futility of war at the **Kaiser-Wilhelm-Gedächtniskirche** (p126) and – assuming it's not Sunday – satisfy your shopping cravings along Kurfürstendamm. Finish at **KaDeWe** (p131) with its mind-boggling food hall.

☼ Spend part of the afternoon absorbing the boho-bourgeois atmosphere of charismatic **Schöneberg** (p132), combing through eclectic boutiques and pausing for a java jolt at **Double Eye** (p133). From Kleistpark catch the U7 to Kottbusser Tor then walk down to the canal and – beer in hand at **Ankerklause** (p96) – watch the boats puttering along.

☾ Dinner options abound around here, be it **Defne** (p92) for upmarket Turkish food, **Horváth** (p92) for Michelin-starred Austrian delights or **Cafe Jacques** (p99) for delicious French-Mediterranean fare. Continue into the night on a bar-hop around **Kottbusser Tor** (p88) or, in fine weather, by heading to **Club der Visionäre** (p94).

Day Four

☼ Pinpoint landmarks you've visited on your first three days from the lofty perch of the **Panoramapunkt** (p61) at Potsdamer Platz before moving on to the **Gemäldegalerie** (p56), a vast museum chock-full with five centuries of paintings by Europe's greatest Old Masters – Rembrandt to Botticelli to Gainsborough.

☼ After lunch at **Qiu** (p66), hop on the U2 and train it to Eberswalder Strasse to embark on a saunter around boho-chic and beautifully gentrified Prenzlauer Berg. Check out the shops and ornate townhouses lining **Kollwitzplatz** (p116) before resting over coffee and cake at **Kaffee Pakolat** (p119). In the mood for more shopping? The indie boutiques and Berlin designer stores along Kastanienallee and Oderberger Strasse should easily hold your interest for another hour or two.

☾ Ring in the evening with a cold Pilsner under the chestnut trees at **Prater** (p118), Berlin's oldest beer garden. Have a sausage here or enjoy a proper German meal around the corner at **Oderquelle** (p117) before heading over to the **Kulturbrauerei** (p120) to catch a concert or play, go dancing or watch a movie.

Need to Know

For more information, see Survival Guide (p173).

Currency
Euro (€)

Language
German (English widely spoken)

Visas
Not required for citizens of the EU, the USA, Canada, Australia and New Zealand (among others) for tourist stays of up to three months.

Money
ATMs widespread. Cash is king in Berlin; credit cards are not widely used.

Mobile Phones
Mobile phones operate on GSM900/1800. If your home country uses a different standard, you'll need a multiband GSM phone. Local SIM cards can be used in European and Australian phones.

Time
Central European Time (GMT/UTC plus one hour).

Plugs & Adaptors
Two-pin plugs running at 230V Ac, 50 Hz. Transformers needed for 110V appliances.

Tipping
Servers 10%, bartenders 5%, taxi drivers 10%, porters €1 to €2 per bag.

Before You Go

Your Daily Budget

Budget less than €50
► Dorm beds €10–20
► Self-catering or fast food

Midrange €50–150
► Double room €80–120
► Two-course dinner with wine €30
► Club cover charge €10–15

Top end more than €150
► 4-star hotel double room €150–200
► Michelin-star dinner with wine €200
► Orchestra seats at the opera €120

Useful Websites

Lonely Planet (www.lonelyplanet.com/berlin) Destination information, hotel bookings, traveller forum and more.

Visit Berlin (www.visitberlin.de) Official tourist authority info.

Museumsportal (www.museumsportal-berlin.de) Gateway to the city's museums.

Resident Advisor (www.residentadvisor.net) Guide to parties and clubbing.

Advance Planning

Two to three months Book tickets for the Berliner Philharmonie, the Staatsoper, Sammlung Boros and top-flight events.

Up to one month Make online reservations for the Reichstag Dome, the Neues Museum and the Pergamonmuseum.

Up to one week Reserve a table at trendy and Michelin-starred restaurants, especially for Friday and Saturday nights.

② Arriving in Berlin

Arrival options in Berlin are changing in 2012 with the opening of Berlin Brandenburg Airport (near the current Schönefeld airport) in June and the subsequent closure of Tegel and the old Schönefeld airports. If arriving by train, Hauptbahnhof is the central station.

✈ From Berlin-Tegel Airport

Destination	Best Transport
Alexanderplatz	TXL express bus
Kurfürstendamm	X9 express bus or bus 109
Kreuzberg – Kottbusser Tor	X9/109 to Ernst-Reuter-Platz, then U8
Brandenburg Gate	TXL express bus

✈ From Berlin-Schönefeld Airport

Destination	Best Transport
Alexanderplatz	Airport-Express train (RB14 or RE7)
Kurfürstendamm	Airport-Express train (RB14 or RE7)
Kreuzberg – Kottbusser Tor	Airport-Express to Alexanderplatz, then U8
Brandenburg Gate	Airport-Express to Alexanderplatz, then bus TXL or 100

✈ From Berlin Brandenburg Airport (from June 2012)

Airport-Express trains (RB14, RE7 and RE9) are expected to depart for central Berlin from the airport's own station every 15 minutes. For the latest information, check www.berlin-airport.de.

🚌 From Hauptbahnhof

Berlin's central train station is served by buses and U-Bahn and S-Bahn trains.

③ Getting Around

Berlin has an extensive and fairly reliable public transport system consisting of the U-Bahn (underground/subway), S-Bahn (light rail), buses and trams. One ticket is good for all forms of transport. For trip planning, see www.bvg.de.

U-Bahn

The most efficient way to travel around Berlin is by U-Bahn, which runs from 4am until about 12.30am and throughout the night on Friday, Saturday and public holidays (all lines except the U4 and U55).

S-Bahn

S-Bahn trains make fewer stops than U-Bahns and are therefore handy for longer distances, but they don't run as frequently. Operating hours are the same.

🚌 Bus

Buses are slower but offer good views. Most run frequently between 4.30am and 12.30am. From Sunday to Thursday, night buses running every 30 minutes take over in intervening hours. MetroBuses (M1, M19) operate 24/7.

🚋 Tram

Trams only operate in the eastern districts. Trams designated M1, M2, etc run 24/7.

🚲 Bicycle

Great for exploring neighbourhoods, cycling is hugely popular in Berlin, which has over 150km of dedicated bike paths. Bikes may be taken into designated carriages of the U-Bahn and S-Bahn. Rental stations are plentiful.

🚕 Taxi

Taxis are fairly inexpensive and come in handy at night when public transport is less frequent. Heavy traffic makes cabs less efficient in the daytime.

Berlin Neighbourhoods

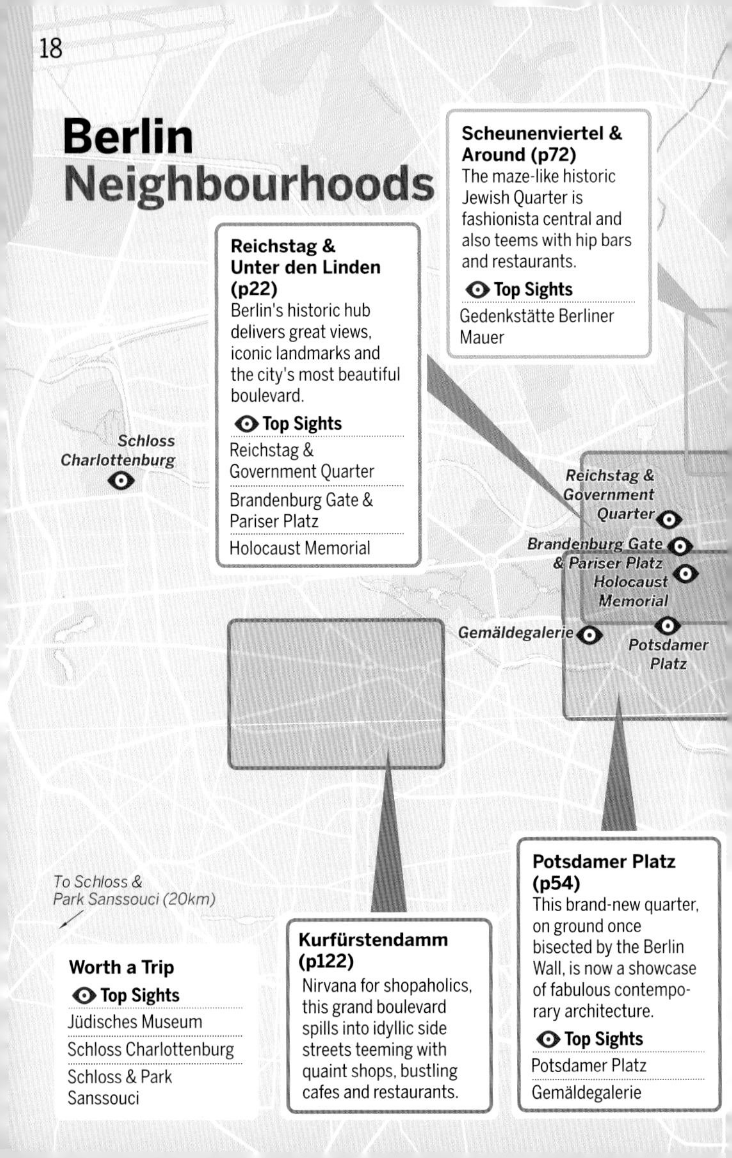

Scheunenviertel & Around (p72)
The maze-like historic Jewish Quarter is fashionista central and also teems with hip bars and restaurants.

⊙ Top Sights
Gedenkstätte Berliner Mauer

Reichstag & Unter den Linden (p22)
Berlin's historic hub delivers great views, iconic landmarks and the city's most beautiful boulevard.

⊙ Top Sights
Reichstag & Government Quarter

Brandenburg Gate & Pariser Platz

Holocaust Memorial

Schloss Charlottenburg ⊙

Reichstag & Government Quarter ⊙

Brandenburg Gate & Pariser Platz ⊙

Holocaust Memorial ⊙

Gemäldegalerie ⊙

Potsdamer Platz ⊙

To Schloss & Park Sanssouci (20km)

Worth a Trip

⊙ Top Sights
Jüdisches Museum

Schloss Charlottenburg

Schloss & Park Sanssouci

Kurfürstendamm (p122)
Nirvana for shopaholics, this grand boulevard spills into idyllic side streets teeming with quaint shops, bustling cafes and restaurants.

Potsdamer Platz (p54)
This brand-new quarter, on ground once bisected by the Berlin Wall, is now a showcase of fabulous contemporary architecture.

⊙ Top Sights
Potsdamer Platz

Gemäldegalerie

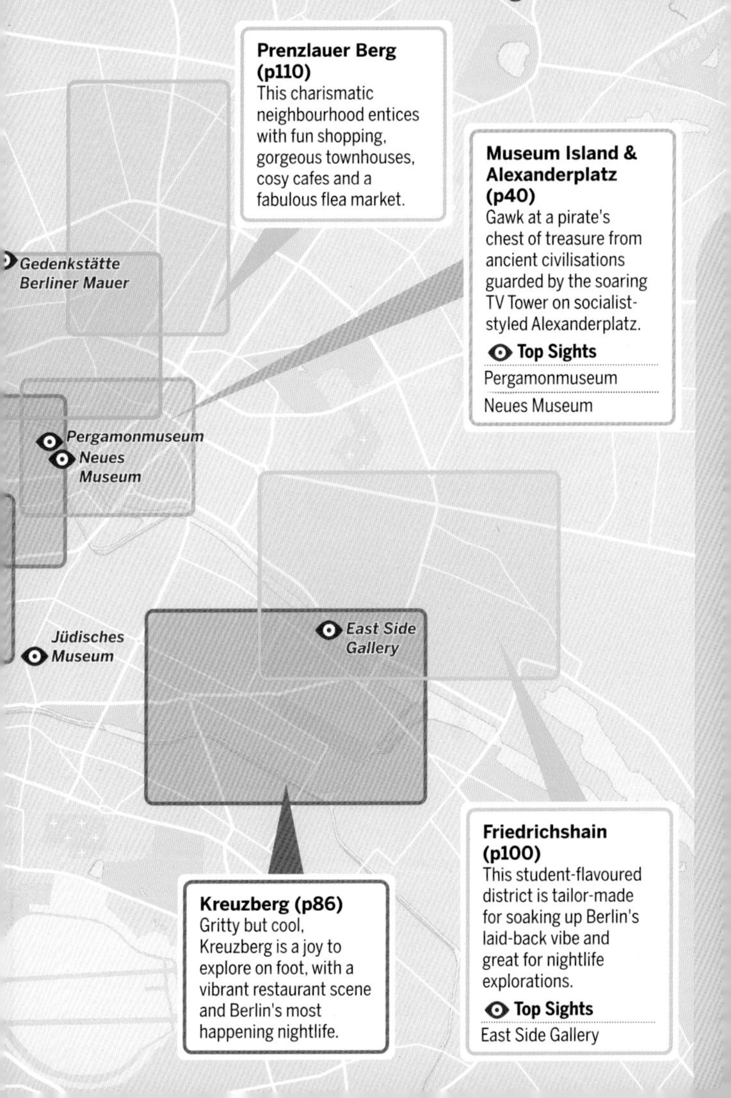

Prenzlauer Berg (p110)
This charismatic neighbourhood entices with fun shopping, gorgeous townhouses, cosy cafes and a fabulous flea market.

Museum Island & Alexanderplatz (p40)
Gawk at a pirate's chest of treasure from ancient civilisations guarded by the soaring TV Tower on socialist-styled Alexanderplatz.

⊙ Top Sights
Pergamonmuseum
Neues Museum

⊙ Gedenkstätte Berliner Mauer

⊙ Pergamonmuseum
⊙ Neues Museum

⊙ East Side Gallery

Jüdisches
⊙ Museum

Friedrichshain (p100)
This student-flavoured district is tailor-made for soaking up Berlin's laid-back vibe and great for nightlife explorations.

⊙ Top Sights
East Side Gallery

Kreuzberg (p86)
Gritty but cool, Kreuzberg is a joy to explore on foot, with a vibrant restaurant scene and Berlin's most happening nightlife.

Explore
Berlin

Worth a Trip

Brandenburg Gate, topped with Quadriga sculpture (p26)
DAVID PEEVERS/LONELY PLANET IMAGES ©

Explore

Reichstag
& Unter den Linden

It's been burned, bombed, rebuilt, buttressed by the Berlin Wall, wrapped in fabric and, finally, adorned with a glass dome: the Reichstag, one of Berlin's most iconic buildings and seat of the German parliament (Bundestag). Nearby, the Brandenburg Gate gives way to Unter den Linden, Berlin's most elegant boulevard, which flaunts its Prussian pedigree with pride.

The Sights in a Day

☀ Book an early time slot for the lift ride up to the **Reichstag** (p24) dome and get the lay of the land while meandering up the spiralling ramp. Back on solid ground, walk a few steps south to snap a classic picture of the **Brandenburg Gate** (p26), then get lost in the haunting maze of the **Holocaust Memorial** (p28). Ponder the source of such evil on the site of **Hitler's bunker** (p33) before strolling over to the **Friedrichstadtpassagen** (p39) for some retail therapy, then lunch at **Augustiner am Gendarmenmarkt** (p36).

☀ Grab a sweet chocolate treat at **Fassbender & Rausch** (p39), take in the architectural harmony of the **Gendarmenmarkt** (pictured left; p32) and follow Friedrichstrasse to Unter den Linden. Head east past Prussian-era beauties for an immersion in German history at the **Deutsches Historisches Museum** (p32). If you still have the time and energy, cap off the afternoon with a spin around the **Tränenpalast** (p32).

☾ To compensate for the meaty lunch at Augustiner, enjoy a gourmet vegetarian dinner at **Cookies Cream** (p36). If it's Tuesday or Thursday hit the dance floor downstairs at **Cookies** (p37); otherwise report to **Bebel Bar** (p37) or **Tausend** (p37) for a nightcap.

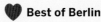

⊙ Top Sights

Reichstag & Government Quarter (p24)

Brandenburg Gate & Pariser Platz (p26)

Holocaust Memorial (p28)

♥ Best of Berlin

Eating
Borchardt (p36)

Fischers Fritz (p35)

Uma (p35)

Cookies Cream (p36)

Bars
Bebel Bar (p37)

Tausend (p37)

Getting There

🚌 **Bus** The 100 and TXL link the Reichstag with Unter den Linden.

S-Bahn The S1 and S2 stop at Brandenburger Tor.

U-Bahn The U55 stops at Bundestag and Brandenburger Tor.

Top Sights
Reichstag & Government Quarter

The nexus of German political power snuggles neatly into the Spreebogen, a horseshoe-shaped bend in the Spree River. The historic anchor of the federal government quarter is the glass-domed Reichstag that once rubbed against the western side of the Berlin Wall. It now forms part of the Band des Bundes (Ribbon of Federal Buildings), a series of glass-and-concrete buildings that symbolically link the former East and West Berlin across the Spree. North of the river looms the solar-panelled Hauptbahnhof (central train station).

◉ Map p30, C2

www.bundestag.de

Platz der Republik 1

admission free

⊘ 8am–midnight, last lift 11pm

U-Bahn Bundestag, Brandenburger Tor; ◨ 100

Don't Miss

Reichstag Building

The four corner towers and mighty facade with the bronze dedication 'Dem Deutschen Volke' (To the German People; added in 1916) are the only original sections of the 1894 Reichstag. Lord Norman Foster, the architectural mastermind of the building's post-reunification makeover, preserved only the historical shell while adding the sparkling glass dome, Berlin's newest symbol.

Reichstag Dome

Whoever said the best things in life are free might have been thinking of the lift ride up to the rooftop of the Reichstag. Enjoy the knockout views, then pick up a free auto-activated audioguide and learn about the building, Berlin landmarks and the workings of the Bundestag while following the ramp spiralling up and around the dome's mirror-clad funnel.

Bundeskanzleramt

Germany's chancellor keeps his or her office in the H-shaped Federal Chancellery designed by Axel Schultes and Charlotte Frank. From Moltkebrücke bridge or the northern Spree River promenade you can best appreciate the circular openings that inspired the building's nickname, 'washing machine'. Eduardo Chillida's rusted-steel *Berlin* sculpture graces the forecourt.

Paul-Löbe-Haus

This vast glass-and-concrete building houses offices for the Bundestag's parliamentary committees. In a visual symbol of reunification, a double footbridge links the building across the Spree to the Marie-Elisabeth-Lüders-Haus, home to the parliamentary library.

☑ Top Tips

▶ Compulsory reservations for visiting the Reichstag dome must be made online at www .bundestag.de. Early booking advised.

▶ Free multilingual audioguides are available on the roof terrace.

▶ Check the website for information on guided tours and attending a plenary session or a lecture on the workings of the Bundestag.

✗ Take a Break

The **Käfer Dachgarten Restaurant** (Map p30, C2; ☎ 2262 9933; www.feinkost -kaefer.de/dachgarten _restaurant; mains lunch €16-24, dinner €25-30) on the Reichstag roof terrace serves gourmet meals; book at least two weeks in advance.

The nearest casual meal is at **Berlin Pavillon** (Map p30, C3; www.berlin-pavillon.de; Scheidemannstrasse 1; mains €2.50-9), a cafeteria/beer garden on the edge of the Tiergarten.

Top Sights
Brandenburg Gate & Pariser Platz

A symbol of division during the Cold War, the landmark Brandenburg Gate (Brandenburger Tor) now epitomises German reunification and often serves as a photogenic backdrop for festivals, mega-concerts and New Year's Eve parties. Carl Gotthard Langhans found inspiration in the Acropolis in Athens for the elegant triumphal arch, completed in 1791 as the royal city gate. It stands sentinel over Pariser Platz, a harmoniously proportioned square once again framed by embassies and bank buildings as it was during its 19th-century heyday.

👁 Map p30, D3

admission free

🕐 24hr

U-/S-Bahn Brandenburger Tor

Don't Miss

Quadriga

Crowning the Brandenburg Gate is Johann Gottfried Schadow's impressive sculpture of the winged goddess of victory piloting a chariot drawn by four horses. After trouncing Prussia in 1806, Napoleon kidnapped the lady and held her hostage in Paris until she was freed by a gallant Prussian general in 1815.

Hotel Adlon

A near-replica of the 1907 original, the Adlon is Berlin's poshest hotel. In 1932 the movie *Grand Hotel,* starring Greta Garbo as a washed-up ballerina, was filmed here. Now called the Adlon Kempinksi, the hotel is still a favourite haunt of the famous, powerful and eccentric. Remember Michael Jackson dangling his baby out the window? It happened at the Adlon.

Museum The Kennedys

Set up like a walk-through family album, this intimate, nonpolitical **museum** (adult/concession €7/3.50; ◷10am-6pm) trains the spotlight on US president John F Kennedy, who has held a special place in German hearts since his *'Ich bin ein Berliner!'* solidarity speech in 1963. Besides photographs, there are various relics, including Jackie's Persian lamb pillbox hat and a hilarious *Superman* comic edition starring the president.

DZ Bank

California-based deconstructivist Frank Gehry masterminded the headquarters of this bank, which packs a visual punch past those bland doors. You'll only get as far as the foyer (open weekdays) but that's enough for a glimpse of the glass-covered atrium with its bizarre free-form sculpture that's actually a conference room.

☑ Top Tips

▶ Pick up maps and information at the tourist office in the gate's south wing.

▶ For a few quiet minutes, pop into the nondenominational meditation room in the gate's north wing.

▶ Sunset and dusk offer the best light conditions for picture-taking.

▶ Check out the schedule of exhibits, readings, lectures and workshops at the Academy of Arts (founded in 1696).

▶ A free exhibition in the Brandenburger Tor U-Bahn station pinpoints milestones in the gate's history.

✗ Take a Break

Head to the Hotel Adlon for coffee and cake, a light lunch or classic afternoon tea.

At dinnertime, try the progressive Asian cuisine at Uma (p35).

Top Sights
Holocaust Memorial

It took 17 years of discussion, planning and construction, but on 10 May 2005 the Memorial to the Murdered Jews of Europe was officially dedicated. Colloquially known as the Holocaust Memorial, it's Germany's central memorial to the Nazi-planned genocide during the Third Reich. For a space the size of a football field, New York architect Peter Eisenman created 2711 sarcophagi-like stelae rising up in sombre silence from undulating ground. You're free to access this labyrinth at any point and make your individual journey through it.

👁 Map p30, D4

www.stiftung-denkmal.de

Ebertstrasse; Info Centre Cora-Berliner-Strasse 1

admission free

🕑24hr; Info Centre 10am-7pm or 8pm

U-/S-Bahn Brandenburger Tor; 🚌200

Don't Miss

Field of Stelae

At first, Peter Eisenman's massive grid of concrete columns of equal size but various heights may seem austere and unemotional, but take time to feel the coolness of the stone and contemplate the interplay of light and shadow. Then plunge into this maze of narrow passageways and give yourself over to a metaphorical sense of disorientation, confusion and claustrophobia.

Ort der Information

If the memorial itself feels rather abstract, the Information Centre movingly lifts the veil of anonymity from the six million Holocaust victims. A graphic timeline of Jewish persecution during the Third Reich is followed by a series of rooms documenting the fates of individuals and families. Poignant and heart-wrenching, these exhibits will leave no one untouched.

Room of Names

In this darkened and most visceral room in the Information Centre, the names and years of birth and death of Jewish victims are projected onto all four walls while a solemn voice reads their short biographies. It takes almost seven years to commemorate all known victims in this fashion.

Homosexuellen Denkmal

In June 2008, the unveiling of the Homosexual Memorial trained the spotlight on the tremendous persecution and suffering of Europe's gay community under the Nazis. Across from the Holocaust Memorial, it's a freestanding 4m-high off-kilter concrete cube designed by Danish-Norwegian artists Michael Elmgreen and Ingar Dragset. A looped video plays through a warped, narrow window.

☑ Top Tips

▶ Free guided tours in English take place at 3pm on Saturday; German tours run at 3pm on Sunday.

▶ Last admission to the Information Centre is 45 minutes before closing.

▶ Audioguides are available for €4 (concession €2).

▶ The memorial is at its moodiest (and most photogenic) when shadows are long, ie early in the morning or late in the day.

✗ Take a Break

Head to nearby **Samādhi** (Map p30, E4; Wilhelmstrasse 77; mains €10-13; ☺lunch & dinner) for curries, satays, soups and noodle dishes, all prepared with fresh vegetables but without meat.

For a wide selection of eating and drinking options, take a short stroll down to Potsdamer Platz (p66).

A B C D

Alt-Moabit

Rahel-Hirsch-Str

Kapelleufer

Spree River

Spreebogenpark

Karlplatz

Willy-Brandt-Str

Moltkebrücke

Otto-von-Bismarck-Allee

Luisenstr

Bundeskanzleramt

Marie-Elisabeth-Lüders-Haus

U Bundestag
Paul-Löbe-Haus

Paul-Löbe-Allee

Reichstag & Government Quarter
◉

Heinrich-Von-Gagern-Str

Platz der Republik

Reichstag

☼ 25

John-Foster-Dulles-Allee

Scheidemannstr

Yitzhak-Rabin-Str

Ebertstr

Pariser Platz

Platz des 18 März

U Brandenburge To

Strasse des 17 Juni

Brandenburg Gate & Pariser Platz
◉ ❶

Cora-Berliner-Str

20 ☕

Tiergartentunnel

Holocaust Memorial ◉

Bellevueallee

Tiergarten

Hannah-Arendt-Str

Hitler's Bunker

In den Ministergärten

Kolmar-Str

Kemperplatz

Lennéstr

Am Park

Ebertstr

Ben-Gurion-Str

Bellevuestr

Vossstr

Leipziger Platz

E
F
G
H

humannstr
Johannisstr

einhardtstr
Ziegelstr
Monbijoustr
Monbijouplatz

1

Marienstr
Albrechtstr
24 ✪
Bertolt-Brecht-Platz
Spree River
Am Weidendamm
Monbijou Park

Am Kupfergraben

MUSEUM ISLAND (MUSEUMSINSEL)

22 🚇
Tränenpalast
3 ◎
Plockstr
Geschwister-Scholl-Str
Spreekanal

Bodestr

19 🚇
Friedrichstr 🚇 23
Georgenstr

chiffbauerdamm
🚇
Bahnhof Friedrichstr
Ⓢ Friedrichstr

2

Reichstagufer
Bauhofstr
Am Zeughaus
Deutsches Historisches Museum

Dorotheenstr
🔒 28
Am Festungs-graben
◎ 21

17 ✖
Mittelstr
Friedrichstr
Charlottenstr
Universitätsstr
10 ◎
Humboldt Universität
5 ◎
◎ 2

Neue Wache
Schlossbrücke

3

Unter den Linden
◎ 9
Oberwallstr
Friedrichs-werdersche Kirche

14 ✖
Deutsche Guggenheim Berlin
4 ◎
27 ✪
Bebelplatz
◎ 8

Behrenstr
Behrenstr
🚇 18

Behrenstr
13 ✖
11 ✖
Französische Str
Kurstr

Französische 🚇 Str
Emil Nolde Museum
◎ 7
Jägerstr

4

Mauerstr
Glinkastr
Jägerstr
30 🔒
26 ✪
15 ✖
1 ◎
Gendarmenmarkt
Taubenstr 🚇 Hausvogteiplatz
Niederwallstr

Taubenstr
Hausvogteiplatz

Mohrenstr
Markgrafenstr
Jerusalemer Str

🚇 Mohrenstr
16 ✖
🔒 29
Kronenstr

5

Wilhelmstr
Stadtmitte 🚇
Ⓝ
0 _____ 400 m
0 _____ 0.2 miles

Leipziger Str

Sights

Gendarmenmarkt   SQUARE

1 ⊙ Map p30, G4

Berlin's most graceful square is bookended by the domed German and French cathedrals and punctuated by the grandly porticoed Konzerthaus Berlin (Concert Hall Berlin; p38). It was named for the Gens d'Armes, an 18th-century Prussian regiment consisting of French Huguenot immigrants whose story is chronicled in a museum inside the French Dome; climb the tower for grand views of historic Berlin. (U-Bahn Französische Strasse)

Deutsches Historisches Museum   MUSEUM

2 ⊙ Map p30, H3

This engaging museum zeroes in on two millennia of German history in all its gore and glory; not in a nutshell but on two floors of a Prussian-era armoury. Check out the Nazi globe, the pain-wrecked faces of dying warrior sculptures in the courtyard, and the temporary exhibits in the boldly modern annexe designed by IM Pei. (German Historical Museum; www.dhm.de; Unter den Linden 2; adult/child €6/free; ⊙10am-6pm; ☒100, 200, TXL)

Tränenpalast   MUSEUM

3 ⊙ Map p30, F2

During the Cold War, tears flowed in this former border shed where East Germans had to bid adieu to family visiting from West Germany – hence its moniker, 'Palace of Tears'. A new exhibit uses original objects, photographs and recordings to grippingly document the division's social impact on the daily lives of Germans on both sides of the border. (Reichstagufer 17; admission free; ⊙9am-7pm Tue-Fri, 10am-6pm Sat & Sun; U-/S-Bahn Friedrichstrasse)

Understand
The Reichstag in History

Germany's federal parliament building has witnessed many milestones in the country's history. After WWI, Philipp Scheidemann proclaimed the German Republic from one of its windows. The Reichstag fire in February 1933 allowed Adolf Hitler to blame the communists and helped catapult him to power. A dozen years later, victorious Red Army troops raised the Soviet flag on the bombed-out building, which stood damaged and empty on the western side of the Berlin Wall throughout the Cold War.

In the '80s, megastars such as David Bowie, Pink Floyd and Michael Jackson performed concerts in front of the building. After the collapse of the Berlin Wall, reunification was enacted in the Reichstag in 1990. Five years later, it made headlines again when the artist couple Christo and Jeanne-Claude wrapped it in fabric. Lord Norman Foster began renovations shortly thereafter.

Bebelplatz SQUARE

4 Map p30, G3

On this treeless square, books by Bertolt Brecht, Thomas Mann, Karl Marx and other 'subversives' went up in flames during the first full-blown public book burning, staged by the Nazi German Student League in 1933. Michael Ullmann's underground installation, *Empty Library,* beneath a glass pane at the square's centre, poignantly commemorates the event. (☐100, 200, TXL)

Neue Wache MEMORIAL

5 Map p30, H3

This columned, temple-like structure, designed by Karl Friedrich Schinkel in 1818, was originally a Prussian royal guardhouse and is now an anti-war memorial. At its centre is Käthe Kollwitz' heart-wrenching sculpture of a mother cradling her dead soldier son. Buried beneath are the remains of an unknown soldier, a resistance fighter and soil from nine European battlefields and concentration camps. (New Guardhouse; Unter den Linden 4; admission free; ☉10am-6pm; ☐100, 200, TXL)

Hitler's Bunker HISTORIC SITE

6 Map p30, D4

Berlin was burning and Soviet tanks advancing relentlessly when Adolf Hitler committed suicide in his bunker on 30 April 1945 alongside Eva Braun, his long-time female companion, hours after their marriage. Today there's just a parking lot and

Christmas market on Gendarmenmarkt

an information panel with a diagram of the vast bunker network, technical data on how it was constructed and information on its post-WWII history. (cnr In den Ministergärten & Gertrud-Kolmar-Strasse; U-/S-Bahn Brandenburger Tor)

Emil Nolde Museum MUSEUM

7 Map p30, G4

Bright flowers, stormy seas and red-lipped women with jaunty hats – the paintings and watercolours of Emil Nolde (1867–1956) are intense, sometimes melancholic and lyrically captivating. Admire a rotating selection of works by this key German expressionist on display in a brightly converted 19th-century bank building. (www.nolde-stiftung.de; Jägerstrasse

Understand

Berlin Under the Swastika

The rise to power of Adolf Hitler and the NSDAP (Nazi Party) in January 1933 had instant and far-reaching consequences for all of Germany. Within three months, all non-Nazi parties, organisations and labour unions had been outlawed and many political opponents, intellectuals and artists detained without trial. Jews, of course, were a main target from the start but the horror escalated during the Kristallnacht pogroms on 9 November 1938, when Nazi thugs desecrated, burned and demolished synagogues and Jewish cemeteries, property and businesses across the country. Jews had begun to emigrate after 1933, but this event set off a stampede.

The fate of those Jews who stayed behind is well known: the systematic, bureaucratic and meticulously documented annihilation in death camps, mostly in Nazi-occupied territories in Eastern Europe. Sinti and Roma (gypsies), political opponents, priests, gays and habitual criminals were targeted as well. Of the roughly seven million people who were sent to concentration camps, only 500,000 survived.

The Battle of Berlin

With the Normandy invasion of June 1944, Allied troops arrived in formidable force on the European mainland, supported by unrelenting air raids on Berlin and most other German cities. The final Battle of Berlin began in mid-April 1945 with 1.5 million Soviet troops barrelling towards the city from the east. On 30 April, when the fighting reached the government quarter, Hitler and his long-time companion Eva Braun committed suicide in their bunker. As their bodies were burning, Red Army soldiers raised the Soviet flag above the Reichstag.

Defeat & Aftermath

The Battle of Berlin ended on 2 May, with Germany's unconditional surrender following six days later. The fighting had taken an enormous toll on Berlin and its people. Much of the city lay in smouldering rubble and at least 125,000 Berliners had lost their lives. In July 1945, the leaders of the Allies met in Potsdam to carve up Germany and Berlin into four zones of occupation controlled by Britain, the USA, the USSR and France.

55; adult/concession €8/3; ⊘10am-7pm; U-Bahn Französische Strasse, Hausvogteiplatz)

Friedrichswerdersche Kirche
CHURCH, MUSEUM

8 ⊙ Map p30, H4

This perkily turreted ex-church by Karl Friedrich Schinkel now shelters 19th-century German sculpture, featuring such period heavyweights as Christian Daniel Rauch and Johann Gottfried Schadow. Upstairs is an exhibit on Schinkel's life and achievements. (www.smb.museum; Werderscher Markt; admission free; ⊘10am-6pm; U-Bahn Hausvogteiplatz)

Deutsche Guggenheim Berlin
GALLERY

9 ⊙ Map p30, G3

A joint venture between Deutsche Bank and the Guggenheim Foundation, this small, minimalist gallery presents themed exhibitions or solo shows starring contemporary art-world hotshots such as Jeff Koons, Hiroshi Sugimoto and Agathe Snow. Nice shop and cafe to boot. (www.deutsche-guggenheim.de; Unter den Linden 13-15; adult/concession €4/3, Mon free; ⊘10am-8pm; U-Bahn Französische Strasse; ⎕100, 200, TXL)

Humboldt Universität
UNIVERSITY

10 ⊙ Map p30, G3

Karl Marx and Friedrich Engels were students, and the Brothers Grimm and Albert Einstein teachers, at Berlin's oldest university (1810), a former royal palace. It has produced enough

Nobel Prize winners (29 at last count) to keep the Swedish Academy busy. These days, some 35,000 students strive to uphold this illustrious legacy.

Eating

Fischers Fritz
INTERNATIONAL €€€

11 Map p30, G4

Even patrons who'd never set foot inside a hotel restaurant must concede that Christian Lohse has earned his two Michelin stars by jazzing up superb fish, meat and seafood into a carnival of flavours. Based at the Regent, Fischers Fritz is formal, so pack your manners. The three-course set lunch for €47 is practically a steal. (☎2033 6363; www.fischersfritzberlin.com; Charlottenstrasse 49; mains €50-90; U-Bahn Französische Strasse)

Uma
ASIAN €€€

12 Map p30, D4

Japanese for 'horse', Uma raises the bar for luxury with its exquisite decor, eye-catching artwork and Euro-inflected Asian dishes that weave flavours together like fine tapestries. Aside from sushi and sashimi, there are meaty mains from the *robata* (charcoal) grill and such tasty morsels as Korean fried octopus and wasabi-infused soft-shell crab meant for sharing. (☎301 117 333; www.uma-restaurant .de; Behrenstrasse 72; mains €15-55; ⊘dinner Mon-Sat; U-/S-Bahn Brandenburger Tor; ⎕100, TXL)

Borchardt
FRANCO-GERMAN €€€

13 ✗ Map p30, F4

A Berlin institution, this high-ceilinged brasserie is as famous for its succulent Wiener schnitzel as it is for its guest roster of international power players, A-list babes and pasty-faced politicians. The neobaroque setting oozes tradition going back to 1853 when the place was founded by the chief caterer to the Prussian royal court. (📞8188 6262; Französische Strasse 47; mains €19-40; U-Bahn Französische Strasse)

Cookies Cream
VEGETARIAN €€€

14 ✗ Map p30, F3

Kudos if you can locate this chic herbivore haven right away. Hint: it's upstairs past a giant chandelier in the service alley of the Westin Grand Hotel. Ring the bell to enter an elegantly industrial loft for flesh-free, flavour-packed dishes from current-harvest ingredients. It's a grand culinary journey that also gets you free admission to Cookies (p37), the eponymous nightclub downstairs. (📞2749 2940; www.cookiescream.com; enter via Behrensstrasse 55; mains €18, 3-course dinner €32; ⏰dinner Tue-Sat; 🍴; U-Bahn Französische Strasse)

Augustiner am Gendarmenmarkt
GERMAN €€

15 ✗ Map p30, G4

Tourists, concert-goers and German-food lovers rub shoulders at rustic tables in Berlin's first authentic Bavarian beer hall. Soak up the down-to-earth vibe right along with a mug of full-bodied Augustiner brew. Sausages, roast pork and pretzels provide rib-sticking sustenance, but there's plenty of lighter (even meat-free) fare as well as good-value lunch specials. (www.augustiner-braeu -berlin.de; Charlottenstrasse 55; mains €6-18; ⏰10am-2am; U-Bahn Französische Strasse)

ChaChà
THAI €€

16 ✗ Map p30, F5

Feeling worn out from sightseeing or power-shopping? No problem: a helping of Massaman curry should quickly return you to top form, for according to the menu of this Thai nosh spot the dish has an 'activating' effect. All menu items here are described to have a 'positive eating' benefit, be it vitalising, soothing or stimulating. Gimmicky? Perhaps, but darn tasty too. (www.eat chacha.com; Friedrichstrasse 63; mains €5-10; ⏰10am-1am; U-Bahn Stadtmitte)

Ishin
JAPANESE €

17 ✗ Map p30, F3

Look beyond the cafeteria-style get-up to sushi glory for minimal wallets. Combination platters are ample and affordable, especially during happy hour, which runs nonstop on Wednesday and Saturday and from 11am to 4pm on other days. Not in the mood for raw fish? Tuck into a steaming rice bowl topped with meat, fish and exotic vegetables. Nice touch: unlimited free green tea. (www.ishin.de, in German; Mittelstrasse 24; platters €7-18; ⏰11am-10pm Mon-Sat; U-/S-Bahn Friedrichstrasse)

Drinking

Cookies
CLUB

This legendary den of dance, downstairs from Cookies Cream (see 14 Map p30, F3), occupies a retro-glam GDR-era cinema tucked within the Westin Grand Hotel building. There's no sign, a tough door and a grown-up ambience. Celeb sightings possible. (www.cookies-berlin.de; Friedrichstrasse 158-164; ⏱Tue, Thu, some Sat; U-Bahn Französische Strasse)

Bebel Bar
BAR

18 Map p30, G3

Channel your inner George Clooney and belly up to the bar at this smooth, mood-lit thirst parlour at the Hotel de Rome. Cocktails here have a progressive, sexy edge that even translates to virgin drinks. Don't bother if you're the whisky-cola type... (Behrenstrasse 37; ⏱from 9am; 🚌100, 200, TXL)

Tausend
BAR

19 Map p30, E2

Beyond an anonymous steel door, flirty frocks sip raspberry mojitos alongside London Mule–cradling three-day stubbles at perhaps the chicest Mitte bar. The contrast between the unceremonious location in the bowels of a railway bridge and the out-of-this-world decor could not be greater. Hungry? Proceed to the 'cantina' in the back room. (www.tausendberlin.com; Schiffbauerdamm 11; ⏱Tue-Sat; U-/S-Bahn Friedrichstrasse)

Felix
CLUB

20 Map p30, D4

Once past the rope of this swanky club at the Adlon (p27), you too can shake your booty to high-octane dance beats, sip champagne cocktails and flirt up a storm. Women get free entry and a glass of Prosecco on Mondays, while the worker-bee brigade kicks loose on after-work Thursdays. (www.felix-clubrestaurant.de; Behrenstrasse 72; ⏱Mon, Thu-Sat; U-/S-Bahn Brandenburger Tor)

Tadschikische Teestube
CAFE

21 Map p30, H3

Sip steaming tea poured from silvery samovars while reclining amid plump pillows, hand-carved sandalwood pillars and heroic murals in this original Tajik tearoom. A 1974 gift from the Soviets to the East German government, it is tucked upstairs in an elegant 18th-century palais that was once a German-Soviet cultural centre. (Am Festungsgraben 1; ⏱5pm-midnight Mon-Fri, from 3pm Sat & Sun; 🚌100, 200, TXL)

Berliner Republik
PUB

22 Map p30, F2

Just as in a mini stock exchange, the cost of drinks fluctuates with demand at this raucous riverside pub. Everyone goes Pavlovian when a heavy brass bell rings, signalling rock-bottom prices. (www.die-berliner-republik .de; Schiffbauerdamm 8; ⏱10am-6am; U-/S-Bahn Friedrichstrasse)

Entertainment

Admiralspalast   THEATRE

23 ⭐ Map p30, F2

This beautifully restored 1920s party palace stages crowd-pleasing plays, concerts and musicals in its elegant historic theatre, and more intimate shows – including comedy, readings, dance, concerts and theatre – on two smaller stages. (☎4799 7499; www.admiralspalast.de, in German; Friedrichstrasse 101-102; U-/S-Bahn Friedrichstrasse)

Berliner Ensemble   THEATRE

24 ⭐ Map p30, E1

The company founded by Bertolt Brecht in 1949 is based at the neo-baroque theatre where his *Threepenny Opera* premiered in 1928. Current artistic director Claus Peymann keeps the master's legacy alive while also peppering the repertory with works by Friedrich Schiller, Heinrich von Kleist and other, mostly classic German,

---

✓ Top Tip

Free Concerts

The gifted students at Berlin's top-rated classical music academy, the **Hochschule für Musik Hanns Eisler** (Map p30, G4; www.hfm-berlin.de; Charlottenstrasse 55), showcase their talents in several recitals weekly, most of them for free or low-cost. They're held either on the main campus or nearby in the Neuer Marstall at Schlossplatz 7.

---

playwrights. (☎2840 8155; www.berliner-ensemble.de, in German; Bertolt-Brecht-Platz 1; U-/S-Bahn Friedrichstrasse)

Haus der Kulturen der Welt   PERFORMING ARTS

25 ⭐ Map p30, A2

This House of World Cultures, in an eccentric building with a gravity-defying parabolic roof, presents the entire palette of contemporary, non-European creativity, from art to music, dance to readings, films to theatre. Chime concerts ring out at noon and 6pm daily from the nearby 68-bell carillon. (www.hkw.de; John-Foster-Dulles-Allee 10; U-Bahn Bundestag; 🚌100; 🛈)

Konzerthaus Berlin   CLASSICAL MUSIC

26 ⭐ Map p30, G4

This top-ranked classical music venue (a Schinkel design from 1821) counts the Konzerthausorchester as its 'house band' but also hosts international artists, thematic concert cycles and children's performances. (☎203 090; www.konzerthaus.de; Gendarmenmarkt 2; U-Bahn Französische Strasse)

Staatsoper Unter den Linden   OPERA

27 ⭐ Map p30, G3

While this historic opera house is under renovation until at least 2014, performances are held at the Schiller Theater in Charlottenburg (see p157). (Unter den Linden 7; U-Bahn Französische Strasse; 🚌100, 200, TXL)

Understand
Bertolt Brecht

Internationally most famous for his 1928 musical play *Die Dreigroschenoper* (Threepenny Opera), Bertolt Brecht (1898–1956) is Germany's most controversial 20th-century poet and playwright. His greatest contribution to drama theory is his creation of 'epic theatre' which, unlike 'dramatic theatre', forces its audience to detach itself emotionally from the play and its characters.

A staunch Marxist, Brecht wrote many of his best plays while in exile in Los Angeles during the Nazi years, most notably *Mother Courage and Her Children* (1941) and *The Good Woman of Setzuan* (1943). He returned to East Berlin in 1949 where he founded the Berliner Ensemble with his wife, actress Helene Weigel.

Shopping

Dussmann – Das Kulturkaufhaus   BOOKS, MUSIC

28 🔒 Map p30, F3

It's easy to lose track of time in this huge book, film and music emporium with reading nooks, a cafe and a performance space used for concerts, political discussions and book readings and signings, usually featuring high-profile authors. (www .kulturkaufhaus.de, in German; Friedrichstrasse 90; ⏱10am-midnight Mon-Fri, to 11.30pm Sat; U-/S-Bahn Friedrichstrasse)

Fassbender & Rausch   FOOD

29 🔒 Map p30, G5

If the Aztecs thought of chocolate as the elixir of the gods, then this depot of truffles and pralines must be heaven. Bonus: the chocolate volcano and the giant model replicas of Berlin landmarks. The upstairs cafe serves sinful chocolate drinks and cakes. (www.fassbender-rausch.de; Charlottenstrasse 60; ⏱10am-8pm Mon-Sat, 11am-8pm Sun; U-Bahn Französische Strasse)

Friedrichstadtpassagen   MALL

30 🔒 Map p30, F4

Get your mitts on international couture, edgy Berlin fashions, gourmet treats and other goodies in this strikingly designed and interlinked trio of ritzy shopping complexes (called *Quartiere*). Highlights are Jean Nouvel's shimmering glass funnel inside the **Galeries Lafayette**, the dazzlingly patterned art-deco-style **Quartier 206**, and John Chamberlain's tower made from crushed automobiles in **Quartier 205**. (Friedrichstrasse 76; U-Bahn Französische Strasse, Stadtmitte)

Explore

Museum Island & Alexanderplatz

Walk through ancient Babylon, meet an Egyptian queen, clamber up a Greek altar or study Monet's moody landscapes. It's treasures galore at Museum Island, a Unesco-recognised cluster of five repositories brimming with art, sculpture and architecture from Europe and beyond. Berlin's medieval birthplace is nearby, serenaded by the spiky TV Tower anchoring noisy, socialist-flavoured Alexanderplatz.

The Sights in a Day

☀️ Beat the crowds by reporting to the **Pergamonmuseum** (p42) before doors open at 10am, then devote at least an hour to checking out the ancient treasures – the Pergamon Altar, the Ishtar Gate etc. Head over to the **Humboldt-Box** (p49) to find out what the fuss is all about with the reconstruction of the Berlin City Palace and to give your camera a workout from the upstairs viewing platform. Follow up with lunch at **Zwölf Apostel** (p52).

☀️ Energy restored, pay your respects to Queen Nefertiti at the **Neues Museum** (p46) or match your interests to any of the other Museum Island contenders. Afterwards, process your impressions during a leisurely **river cruise** (p50) through Berlin's historic centre, then get a bird's-eye view of the city from the top of **TV Tower** (pictured left with the Berliner Dom; p50), Germany's tallest structure.

🌙 If you want an old-timey dinner experience, wrap up the day with a traditional German meal at **Zur Letzten Instanz** (p52); for edgier flair, book a table at **.HBC** (p52), whose bar is also a fine place for a nightcap.

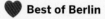

👁️ Top Sights

💜 Best of Berlin

Getting There

🚌 **Bus** The 100, 200 and TXL link Alexanderplatz with Museum Island.

S-Bahn The S5, S7/75 and S9 all converge at Alexanderplatz. For Museum Island, Hackescher Markt and Friedrichstrasse stations are closer.

🚊 **Tram** The M1 and 12 stop at Am Kupfergraben west of Museum Island.

U-Bahn The U2, U5 and U8 stop at Alexanderplatz. Friedrichstrasse is the closest station to Museum Island.

Top Sights
Pergamonmuseum

Berlin's top tourist attraction, the Pergamonmuseum is an Aladdin's cave of treasures that opens up a fascinating window into the ancient world. Inside the palatial three-wing complex, custom-built on Museum Island and open since 1930, awaits a rich feast of classical sculpture and monumental architecture from Greece, Rome, Babylon and the Middle East, most famously the namesake altar from Pergamon. Most of it was excavated and spirited to Berlin by German archaeologists at the turn of the 20th century.

⊙ Map p48, A2

www.smb.museum

Am Kupfergraben 5

adult/concession €10/5

⊙10am-6pm, to 10pm Thu

🚌100, 200, TXL; S-Bahn Hackescher Markt; U-Bahn Friedrichstrasse; 🚊M1, 12

Pergamon Altar

Don't Miss

Pergamon Altar

The museum's namesake cuts a commanding presence in the first hall you enter. This massive 2nd-century-BC marble shrine hails from the Greek metropolis of Pergamon (now Bergama in Turkey) and centres on a steep and wide staircase. Climb up to a colonnaded courtyard adorned with a vivid frieze featuring episodes from the life of Telephos, Pergamon's mythical founder.

Pergamon Frieze

Reconstructed along the walls of the altar hall is another, even more impressive, frieze. About 113m long, it shows the gods locked in an epic battle with the giants. It was originally a painted and gilded band wrapped around the entire shrine. The anatomical detail, the emotional intensity and the dramatic composition of the figures show Hellenic art at its finest.

Pergamon Panorama

Yadegar Asisi's dizzyingly detailed 360-degree 25m-high **Pergamon Panorama** (www.pergamon -panorama.de; adult/concession €13/8.50, combination tickets available; ⊙9am-6pm, to 9pm Thu) helps you visualise antique Pergamon on a random day in 129 AD. Barking dogs, chirping birds and a day-to-night simulation enhance the theatrical experience that's on view in its own temporary rotunda in the museum's forecourt until 30 September 2012.

Pergamon Special Exhibit

Also until September 2012, rarely exhibited sculptures, mosaics, tools, musical instruments and other objects illustrate way stations and aspects of ancient Pergamon. Life under

☑ Top Tips

▶ Avoid the worst crowds by arriving early or late on weekdays.

▶ Skip the queue by buying tickets online in advance.

▶ Pick up the excellent free audioguide.

▶ The Pergamon Pass (adult/concession €18/15) is good for admission to the Pergamon Panorama and the museum's permanent and special exhibits.

▶ The Museumsinsel 'area ticket' (€14/7) is valid for one-time, same-day admission to the permanent exhibits of the Pergamonmuseum, Altes Museum, Bodemuseum, Alte Nationalgalerie and Neues Museum.

✗ Take a Break

Refuel at **Cafe Pergamon** (mains €4-10) in the museum's north wing.

Nearby, Zwölf Apostel (p52) has lunchtime pizza specials.

Greek, Roman and Attalid rule; the cult around Athena; temples and sanctuaries and funeral rites are all addressed.

Market Gate of Miletus

Merchants and customers once flooded through this splendid 17m-high gate into the bustling market square of Miletus, a key Roman trading town in today's Turkey. Destroyed by an earthquake in the 11th century, the richly decorated marble gate blends Greek and Roman design features and was probably built to welcome Emperor Hadrian on his 126 AD visit to Miletus.

Ishtar Gate

Expect your jaw to drop as you face the magnificence of the reconstructed Babylonian town gate, Processional Way and facade of the throne hall of its builder, King Nebuchadnezzar II (604–562 BC). Walls are sheathed in radiant blue and ochre glazed bricks with friezes of strutting lions, bulls and dragons representing Babylonian gods. They're so striking you can almost imagine hearing the roaring and fanfare.

Stela of Hammurabi

Back in the 18th century BC, King Hammurabi of Babylon decided to assert his royal authority by having his law decrees carved into an imposing stela (upright stone slab), a copy of which anchors the Babylonian Hall. Despite

Pergamonmuseum

Ground Floor

Upper Floor

Understand
Museum Island Master Plan

The Pergamonmuseum is part of Museum Island (Museumsinsel), a cluster of five repositories that collectively became a Unesco World Heritage Site in 1999. The distinction was at least partly achieved because of a master plan that will link four of the five buildings by a subterranean passageway decorated with archaeological objects. Masterminded by British architect David Chipperfield, the complex will eventually be entered through a colonnaded modern foyer named for early-20th-century German-Jewish philanthropist James Simon. Learn more at www .museumsinsel-berlin.de.

Aleppo Room

Guests arriving in this richly painted, wood-panelled reception room would have had no doubt of the wealth and power of its owner, a Christian merchant in 17th-century Aleppo, Syria. The beautiful, if dizzying, decorations combine Islamic floral and geometric motifs with courtly scenes and Christian themes. Look closely to make out *The Last Supper* to the right of the central door.

Rock Crystal Ewer

Glass breaks all too easily, which is what makes this 1000-year-old perfectly preserved rock crystal ewer from Egypt such a rare and special piece. Note the finely balanced shape and the intricate decoration featuring chained cheetahs, a symbol of the Fatimid caliphs. The enamelled gold encasing was added in the 19th century.

their ancient pedigree, some of the phrases are still heard today, including 'an eye for an eye; a tooth for a tooth'.

Caliph's Palace of Mshatta

When Ottoman Sultan Abdul Hamid II wanted to get into Emperor Wilhelm II's good graces, he gave him a most generous gift: the facade of the 8th-century palace of Mshatta in today's Jordan. A masterpiece of early Islamic art, it depicts animals and mythical creatures frolicking peacefully amid a riot of floral motifs in an allusion to the Garden of Eden.

Top Sights
Neues Museum

David Chipperfield's reconstruction of the bombed-out New Museum on Museum Island is the new home of the show-stopping Egyptian Museum (headlined by Queen Nefertiti) and the equally enthralling Museum of Pre- and Early History. Like a giant jigsaw puzzle, the British star architect incorporated every original shard, scrap and brick he could find into the new structure. This brilliant blend of the historic and modern creates a dynamic space that beautifully juxtaposes massive stairwells, domed rooms, murralled halls and high ceilings.

👁 Map p48, B3

www.neues-museum.de

Bodestrasse 1

adult/concession €10/5

🕙10am-6pm Sun-Wed, to 8pm Thu-Sat

🚌100, 200, TXL; S-Bahn Hackescher Markt; U-Bahn Friedrichstrasse; 🚋M1, 12

Egyptian reliefs at the Neues Museum

Don't Miss

Nefertiti

An audience with Berlin's most beautiful woman, the 3330-year-old Queen Nefertiti – she of the long graceful neck and timeless good looks – is a must. The bust was part of the treasure trove unearthed by a Berlin expedition of archaeologists around 1912 while sifting through the sands of Armana, the royal city built by Nefertiti's husband, King Akhenaten.

Berliner Goldhut

Resembling a wizard's hat, the 3000-year-old Berlin Gold Hat must indeed have struck the Bronze Age people as something magical. The entire cone is swathed in elaborate bands of astrological symbols believed to have helped priests calculate the movements of sun and moon and thus predict the best times for planting and harvesting. It's one of only four unearthed worldwide.

Berlin Grüner Kopf

A key item from the Late Egyptian Period, which shows Greek influence, is the so-called Berlin 'Green Head' (c 400 BC), the bald head of a priest carved from smooth green stone. Unusual for art from this period, the sculptor did not create a realistic portrait of a specific person but rather sought to convey universal wisdom and experience.

Trojan Collection

Three humble-looking silver jars are the star exhibits among the Trojan antiquities discovered by archaeologist Heinrich Schliemann in 1870 near Hisarlik in today's Turkey. Many other objects on display, including elaborate jewellery, ornate weapons and gold mugs, are replicas since the originals were looted by the Soviets after WWII and remain in Moscow to this day.

☑ Top Tips

▶ Skip the queue by buying tickets online in advance.

▶ Museum tickets are only valid for admission during a designated half-hour time slot.

▶ Tours (€5) focusing on the museum's history and architecture take place at 6pm Thursday and Friday.

▶ The Museumsinsel 'area ticket' (€14/7) is valid for one-time, same-day admission to the Neues Museum as well as the Altes Museum, Bodemuseum, Alte Nationalgalerie and Pergamonmuseum.

✗ Take a Break

The lure of potent java and homemade snacks keeps the on-site **Allegretto Museumscafe** (dishes €2-9) abuzz.

Sights

Altes Museum   MUSEUM

1 ◎ Map p48, B3

Designed by Karl Friedrich Schinkel, this grand, column-fronted museum with its Pantheon-inspired rotunda is a majestic backdrop for Greek, Etruscan and Roman art and sculpture. A statue of a seated goddess from Tarent stands out from among the many vases, bronzes, tomb reliefs, weapons and jewellery going back as far as 6000 years to the Minoans. Adults-only: the upstairs 'Erotic Cabinet'. (Old Museum; www.smb.museum; Am Lustgarten; adult/concession €8/4; ☺10am-6pm, to 10pm Thu; S-Bahn Hackescher Markt; ⬛100, 200, TXL)

DDR Museum   MUSEUM

2 ◎ Map p48, B3

How did regular East German Joes and Janes spend their day-to-day lives? This 'touchy-feely' museum does a delightful job at pulling back the Iron Curtain on an extinct society. You get to squeeze behind the wheel of a tinny Trabant car, rummage through a schoolbag, watch East German TV and find out why kids were put through collective potty training. (GDR Museum; www.ddr-museum.de; Karl-Liebknecht-Strasse 1; adult/concession €6/4; ☺10am-8pm, to 10pm Sat; ⬛100, 200, TXL)

Humboldt-Box   MUSEUM

3 ◎ Map p48, B3

This oddly shaped structure offers a sneak preview of the planned reconstruction of the Berlin City Palace, to be known as Humboldt-Forum. The Box displays teasers from each future resident – the Ethnological Museum, the Museum of Asian Art and the Central Library – along with a fantastically detailed model of the historic city centre. Great views from the upstairs terrace. (www.humboldt-box .com; Schlossplatz; adult/concession €4/2.50; ☺10am-8pm; ⬛100, 200, TXL)

Understand
Reconstruction of the Berlin City Palace

Starting in 2014, Germany's most ambitious, costly and controversial cultural construction project will kick off on Schlossplatz: the rebuilding of the Berlin City Palace that stood in the vast empty space (now overlooked by the Humboldt-Box) for nearly 500 years. Although barely war-damaged, the East German government demolished it in 1951 and replaced it with an asbestos-riddled multipurpose hall called Palace of the Republic, which itself met the wrecking ball in 2008. The future doppelgänger palace, which will have a historical facade coupled with a modern interior, will house a cultural centre known as Humboldt-Forum.

TV Tower
LANDMARK

4 ⊙ Map p48, D2

Berlin's iconic TV Tower – Germany's tallest structure – has been soaring 368m high since 1969. On clear days, views from the panorama platform are stunning. Savour them – refreshment in hand – in the lovably stuffy, slowly revolving restaurant-bar. VIP ticket holders can jump the queue. (Fernsehturm; www.tv-turm.de; Panoramastrasse 1a; adult/child €19.50/11.50; ⊙9am-midnight Mar-Oct, from 10am Nov-Feb; U-/S-Bahn Alexanderplatz)

Berliner Dom
CHURCH

5 ⊙ Map p48, B3

Pompous yet majestic, the former royal court church (1905) does triple duty as house of worship, museum

---

☑️ Top Tip

Sightseeing River Cruises

A lovely way to experience Berlin from April to October – and a great break from museum-hopping – is from the open-air deck of a river cruiser. Several companies run relaxing one-hour (about €9) Spree spins through the city centre from landing docks just north of Museum Island. Sip refreshments while a guide showers you with tidbits (in English and German) as you glide past grand old buildings, beach bars and the government quarter.

---

and concert hall. The 7269-pipe Sauer organ and the elaborate sarcophagi made for various royals are top draws. Climb the 267 steps to the gallery for glorious city views. (Berlin Cathedral; www.berliner-dom.de; Am Lustgarten; adult/child/concession €7/free/4, audioguide €3; ⊙9am-8pm Mon-Sat, noon-8pm Sun Apr-Sep, to 7pm Oct-Mar; 🚌100, 200, TXL)

Bodemuseum
MUSEUM

6 ⊙ Map p48, A2

This neobaroque Museum Island beauty shelters Byzantine art, 2700 years worth of coins and, most importantly, a priceless collection of European sculpture by such artists as Donatello, Bernini and Tilmann Riemenschneider. (www.smb.museum; Am Kupfergraben 1; adult/concession €8/4; ⊙10am-6pm, to 10pm Thu; S-Bahn Hackescher Markt, Oranienburger Strasse)

Alte Nationalgalerie
GALLERY

7 ⊙ Map p48, B2

This Greek-temple building on Museum Island showcases top-notch 19th-century European art, including Caspar David Friedrich's mystical landscapes, Max Liebermann's portraits and Adolph Menzel's epic glorifications of Prussian military might. (Old National Gallery; www.smb.museum; Bodestrasse 1-3; adult/concession incl audioguide €10/5; ⊙10am-6pm Tue, Wed & Fri-Sun, to 10pm Thu; S-Bahn Hackescher Markt; 🚌100, 200, TXL)

Understand

Red Berlin: Life in the GDR

Two Germanys

The formal division of Germany in 1949 resulted in the western zones becoming the Bundesrepublik Deutschland (BRD; Federal Republic of Germany, FRG) with Bonn as its capital, and the Soviet zone morphing into the Deutsche Demokratische Republik (DDR; German Democratic Republic, GDR) with East Berlin as its capital. Despite the latter's name, only one party – the Sozialistische Einheitspartei Deutschlands (SED; Socialist Unity Party of Germany) – controlled all policy until 1989.

The Stasi

In order to oppress any opposition, the GDR government established the Ministry for State Security (Stasi) in 1950 and put millions of its own citizens under surveillance. Tactics included wire-tapping, videotape observation and the opening of private mail. Real or suspected regime critics often ended up in Stasi-run prisons. The organisation grew steadily in power and size, and by the end had 91,000 official full-time employees plus 173,000 informants. The latter were recruited among regular folk to spy on their co-workers, friends, family and neighbours as well as on people in West Germany.

Economic Woes & the Wall

While West Germany blossomed in the 1950s, thanks to the US-sponsored Marshall Plan economic aid package, East Germany stagnated, partly because of the Soviets' continued policy of asset stripping and reparation payments. As the economic gulf widened, scores of mostly young and educated East Germans decided to seek a future in the west, further straining the economy and leading to the construction of the Berlin Wall in 1961 to stop the exodus. (Read more about it on p65.)

The appointment of Erich Honecker in 1971 opened the way for rapprochement with the west. Honecker fell in line with Soviet politics but his economic approach did improve the East German economy, eventually leading to the collapse of the regime and the fall of the Berlin Wall in November 1989.

Eating

.HBC

INTERNATIONAL €€€

8 🍴 Map p48, C2

This multitasking bar-gallery-concert-party venue in the former Hungarian cultural centre also has a respectable restaurant that lures adventurous eaters with exciting flavour pairings (think foie gras flan or an octopus, chorizo and port wine fry-up). Take in the charmingly socialist retro ambience while glimpsing the TV Tower through the picture windows. (📞2434 2920; www.hbc-berlin.de; Karl-Liebknecht-Strasse 9; mains €15-18; ⏰from 7pm Mon-Sat; U-/S-Bahn Alexanderplatz)

Brauhaus Georgbräu

INTERNATIONAL €€

9 🍴 Map p48, C4

Tourist-geared but cosy, this brewpub is the only place where you can guzzle the locally made St Georg Pilsner. In winter the woodsy beer hall is perfect for tucking into hearty Berlin-style goulash or *Eisbein* (boiled pork knuckle), while in summer the riverside beer garden beckons. (www.georgbraeu.de; Spreeufer 4; mains €10-14; U-/S-Bahn Alexanderplatz)

Zur Letzten Instanz

GERMAN €€

10 🍴 Map p48, E4

Oozing folksy Old Berlin charm, this rustic eatery has been an enduring hit since 1621 and has fed everyone from Napoleon to Beethoven to Angela Merkel. Quality is pretty high when it comes to such rib-stickers as *Grillhaxe* (grilled pork knuckle) and *Bouletten* (meat patties). (📞242 5528; www.zur letzteninstanz.de; Waisenstrasse 14-16; ⏰Mon-Sat; U-Bahn Klosterstrasse)

Zwölf Apostel

PIZZERIA €€

11 🍴 Map p48, A2

A pleasant pit stop between museums, this place beneath the railway arches has over-the-top religious decor and tasty thin-crust pizzas named after the 12 apostles. All cost a mere €6.95 from 11.30am to 4pm Monday to Friday. (www.12-apostel.de, in German; Georgenstrasse 2; pizzas €8-18; U-/S-Bahn Friedrichstrasse; 🚃M1, 12)

Berliner Dom and TV Tower (p50)

Drinking

Weekend
CLUB

12 🍷 Map p48, E2

At this high-flying house and techno dancing den, star DJs whip shiny, happy hotties into a frenzy. Watching the sunrise from the rooftop bar is a transcendent summer experience, and even Alexanderplatz looks great through the huge 12th-floor panoramic windows. Meanwhile, in the jet-black bat cave on the 15th floor you can pretend that the night will never end. (www.week-end-berlin.de; Am Alexanderplatz 5; ⏱Thu-Sat; U-/S-Bahn Alexanderplatz)

Strandbar Mitte
BEER GARDEN

13 🍷 Map p48, A2

Alas, the sand has been replaced with asphalt at Berlin's original beach bar, but the riverfront setting and front-row views of the Bodemuseum on Museum Island still make Strandbar a summertime fave. There's thin-crust pizza for noshing and live comedic plays in the adjacent amphitheatre. (www.strandbar-mitte.de; Monbijoustrasse 3; ⏱from 10am Apr-Sep; S-Bahn Hackescher Markt)

Shopping

Ausberlin
GIFTS, SOUVENIRS

14 🔒 Map p48, D2

'Made in Berlin' is the motto of this low-key store where you can pick up the latest BPitch or Ostgut CD, witty Kotty D'Azur T-shirts by Muschi Kreuzberg, a Bar 25 pillow and all sorts of other hot-label mementoes designed right here in this fair city. (www.ausberlin.de, in German; Karl-Liebknecht-Strasse 17; ⏱10am-7pm Mon-Sat; U-/S-Bahn Alexanderplatz)

Alexa
MALL

15 🔒 Map p48, E3

Power-shoppers love this XXL-sized mega-mall near Alexanderplatz. Besides the usual mainstream retailers, there's a store by German rapper Bushido, and Loxx, the world's largest model railway. Good food court to boot. (www.alexacentre.com, in German; Grunerstrasse 20; ⏱10am-9pm Mon-Sat; U-/S-Bahn Alexanderplatz)

Explore

Potsdamer Platz

Despite the name, Potsdamer Platz is not just a square but Berlin's newest quarter, birthed in the '90s from terrain once bisected by the Berlin Wall. A collaborative effort by the world's finest architects, it is a vibrant showcase of urban renewal. A visit here is easily combined with the Kulturforum, a cluster of top-notch museums and concert halls, including the world-famous Berliner Philharmonie.

The Sights in a Day

☼ Start the day with buttery croissants and homemade jam at **Desbrosses** (p66), then whiz up to the top of the **Panoramapunkt** (p61) for bird's-eye views of Berlin's landmarks. Check out the shops at the **Potsdamer Platz Arkaden** (p67) on your way to the **Gemäldegalerie** (p56) for your rendezvous with Rembrandt & co. Once you've exhausted your attention span, head back to Potsdamer Platz and join the business brigade for a delicious lunch at **Qiu** (p66).

☼ Thus fortified, it's time to take a closer look at the futuristic architecture of the **Sony Center** (pictured left; p61). Spend the afternoon delving first into the darkness of the Nazi era at the **Topographie des Terrors** (p63) and then the Cold War at **Checkpoint Charlie** (p63). By now you're probably ready for a drink, so head to **Solar** (p66) for libations with a view.

☾ Grab an early dinner at **Vapiano** (p66), then wrap up the day with a bit of culture by taking in a classical concert at the **Berliner Philharmonie** (p67).

👁 Top Sights

Potsdamer Platz (p60)

Gemäldegalerie (p56)

♥ Best of Berlin

Historical Sites
Topographie des Terrors (p63)

Gedenkstätte Deutscher Widerstand (p64)

Checkpoint Charlie (p63)

Art
Gemäldegalerie (p56)

Neue Nationalgalerie (p64)

DaimlerContemporary (p61)

Berliner Philharmonie (p67)

Live Music
Berliner Philharmonie (p67)

Getting There

🚌 **Bus** The 200 comes from Zoologischer Garten and Alexanderplatz, the M41 from the Hauptbahnhof and the M29 from Checkpoint Charlie.

S-Bahn The S1 and S2 stop at Potsdamer Platz.

U-Bahn Handy stops on the U2 include Potsdamer Platz and Mendelssohn-Bartholdy-Park.

Top Sights
Gemäldegalerie

When the Picture Gallery, Berlin's grand survey of Old Masters, opened in its custom-built Kulturforum space in 1998, it marked the happy reunion of an outstanding collection of European paintings separated by the Cold War for half a century. About 1500 works span the arc of artistic vision between the 13th and 18th centuries. Rooms radiating out from the football-field-sized central foyer brim with key canvases by Rembrandt, Titian, Goya, Botticelli, Holbein, Gainsborough, Canaletto, Hals, Rubens, Vermeer and other heavy hitters.

◉ Map p62, A3

www.smb.museum

Matthaïkirchplatz 8

adult/concession €8/4

🕙 10am-6pm Tue, Wed & Fri-Sun, to 10pm Thu

U-/S-Bahn Potsdamer Platz; 🚍 M29, 200

Dutch Proverbs (1559) by Pieter Bruegel the Elder

Don't Miss

Amor Victorius (1602–03)
ROOM XIV

That's quite a cheeky fellow peering down on viewers, isn't it? Wearing nothing but a mischievous grin and a pair of black angel wings, with a fistful of arrows, this Amor means business. In this famous painting, Caravaggio shows off his amazing talent at depicting objects with near-photographic realism achieved by his ingeniously theatrical use of light and shadow.

Dutch Proverbs (1559)
ROOM 7

In this moralistic yet humorous painting, Dutch Renaissance painter Pieter Bruegel the Elder manages to illustrate over 100 proverbs and idioms in a single seaside village scene. While some emphasise the absurdity of human behaviour, others unmask its imprudence and sinfulness. Some sayings are still in use today, among them 'swimming against the tide' and 'armed to the teeth'.

Portrait of Hieronymus Holzschuher (1526)
ROOM 2

Hieronymus Holzschuher was a Nuremberg patrician, a career politician and a strong supporter of the Reformation. He was also a friend of one of the greatest German Renaissance painters, Albrecht Dürer. In this portrait, which shows its sitter at age 57, the artist brilliantly lasers in on Holzschuher's features with utmost precision, down to the furrows, wrinkles and thinning hair.

Woman with a Pearl Necklace (1662–64)
ROOM 18

No, it's not the *Girl with a Pearl Earring* of book and movie fame, but it's still one of Jan

☑ Top Tips

▶ Take advantage of the excellent free audioguide to get the low-down on selected works.

▶ A tour of all 72 rooms covers almost 2km, so budget at least a couple of hours for your visit and wear comfortable shoes.

▶ Admission is free to anyone under 18.

▶ A ticket to the Gemäldegalerie is also good for same-day admission to the permanent collections of the other Kulturforum museums.

✗ Take a Break

The upstairs cafeteria at the museum has a salad bar, pre-cooked meals (around €6) and hot and cold beverages.

A short walk away around Potsdamer Platz are Weilands Wellfood (p66) and several other eating options.

Vermeer's most famous paintings: a young woman studies herself in the mirror while fastening a pearl necklace. A top dog among Dutch Realist painters, Vermeer mesmerises viewers by beautifully capturing this intimate moment with characteristic soft brushstrokes.

Fountain of Youth (1546)
ROOM III

Lucas Cranach the Elder's poignant painting illustrates humankind's yearning for eternal youth. Old crones plunge into a pool of water and emerge as dashing hotties – this fountain would surely put plastic surgeons out of business. The transition is also reflected in the landscape, which is stark and craggy on the left, and lush and fertile on the right.

Malle Babbe (1633)
ROOM 13

Frans Hals ingeniously captures the character and vitality of his subject, 'Crazy Barbara', with free-wielding brushstroke. Hals met the lady with the almost demonic laugh in the workhouse for the mentally ill where his son Pieter was also a resident. The tin mug and owl are symbols of Babbe's fondness for tipple.

Leda with the Swan (1532)
ROOM XVI

Judging by her blissed-out expression, Leda is having a fine time with that swan who, according to Greek

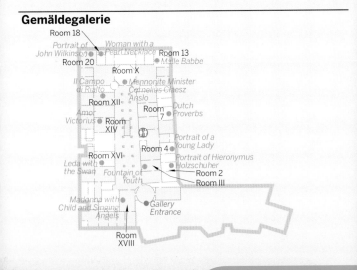

Gemäldegalerie

Room 18
Portrait of John Wilkinson
Woman with a Pearl Necklace
Room 20
Room 13
Malle Babbe
Room X
Il Campo di Rialto
Mennonite Minister Cornelius Claesz Anslo
Room XII
Room 7
Dutch Proverbs
Amor Victorius
Room XIV
Portrait of a Young Lady
Room XVI
Room 4
Portrait of Hieronymus Holzschuher
Leda with the Swan
Fountain of Youth
Room 2
Room III
Madonna with Child and Singing Angels
Gallery Entrance
Room XVIII

mythology, is none other than Zeus himself. The erotically charged nature of this painting by Italian Renaissance artist Correggio apparently so incensed Louis, duke of Orleans, that he cut off Leda's head with a knife. It was later restored by Jacob Schlesinger.

Portrait of a Young Lady (1470)
ROOM 4

Berlin's own 'Mona Lisa' may not be as famous as the real thing but she's quite intriguing nonetheless. Who is this woman with the almond-shaped eyes and porcelain skin who gazes straight at us with a blend of sadness and scepticism? This famous portrait is a key work by Petrus Christus and his only one depicting a woman.

Madonna with Child and Singing Angels (1477)
ROOM XVIII

Renaissance artist Sandro Botticelli's circular painting (a format called a *tondo*) is a symmetrical composition showing Mary at the centre flanked by two sets of four wingless angels. It's an intimate moment that shows the Virgin tenderly embracing – perhaps even about to breastfeed – her child. The white lilies are symbols of her purity.

Mennonite Minister Cornelius Claesz Anslo (1641)
ROOM X

A masterpiece in the gallery's prized Rembrandt collection, this large-scale canvas shows the cloth merchant and Mennonite preacher Anslo in conversation with his wife. The huge open Bible and his gesturing hand sticking out in almost 3D style from the centre of the painting are meant to emphasise the strength of his religious convictions.

Portrait of John Wilkinson (1775)
ROOM 20

Works by Thomas Gainsborough are rarely seen outside the UK, which is what makes this portrait of British industrialist John Wilkinson so special. Nicknamed 'Iron Mad Wilkinson' for pioneering the making and use of cast iron, here he is – somewhat ironically – shown in a natural setting, almost blending in with his surroundings.

Il Campo di Rialto (1758–63)
ROOM XII

Giovanni Antonio Canal, aka Canaletto, studied painting in the workshop of his theatre-set designer father. Here he depicts the Campo di Rialto, the arcaded main market square of his hometown Venice, with stunning precision and perspective. Note the goldsmith shops on the left, the wig-wearing merchants in the centre and the stores selling paintings and furniture on the right.

Top Sights
Potsdamer Platz

Potsdamer Platz 2.0 is essentially a modern re-interpretation of the historic original, which was the equivalent of New York's Times Square until WWII sucked all life out of the area. It's divided into three slices: DaimlerCity with a large mall, public art and high-profile entertainment venues; the flashy Sony Center built around a central plaza canopied by a glass roof that shimmers in myriad colours at night; and the comparatively subdued Beisheim Center, which was inspired by classic American skyscraper design.

👁 Map p62, C2

www.potsdamerplatz.de

U-/S-Bahn Potsdamer Platz

Roof of the Sony Center by night

Don't Miss

Panoramapunkt
Europe's fastest **lift** (www.panoramapunkt.de; Potsdamer Platz 1; adult/concession €5.50/4; ☺10am-8pm) yo-yos up and down the red-brick post-modern Kollhof Building. From the 100m viewing platform, a stunning 360-degree panorama reveals the city layout and its landmarks. Study key moments in Potsdamer Platz history by taking in the exhibit, then relax over coffee in the on-site cafe.

Sony Center
Helmut Jahn's visually dramatic Sony Center is fronted by a 26-floor glass-and-steel tower that integrates rare relics from the pre-war Potsdamer Platz. These include a section of facade of the Hotel Esplanade and the opulent Kaisersaal hall, whose 75m move to its current location required some wizardly technology. Enjoy a spot of people-watching in the cafe-flanked central plaza.

Museum für Film und Fernsehen
This Sony Center **museum** (www.deutsche -kinemathek.de; adult/concession €6/4.50; ☺10am-6pm Tue, Wed & Fri-Sun, to 8pm Thu) charts milestones in German film and TV history. The most engaging galleries are those dedicated to pioneers such as Fritz Lang, groundbreaking movies such as Leni Riefenstahl's *Olympia,* German exiles in Hollywood and diva extraordinaire Marlene Dietrich.

Weinhaus Huth
The 1912 Weinhaus Huth, one of the first steel-frame buildings in town, was the only Potsdamer Platz structure to survive WWII intact. On the top floor, the **DaimlerContemporary** (www .sammlung.daimler.com; admission free; ☺11am-6pm) showcases international abstract, conceptual and minimalist art. Ring the bell to be buzzed in.

☑ Top Tips
▶ Check out the Berlin Wall segments outside the Potsdamer Platz station entrance.

▶ Keep an eye out for public sculptures by Keith Haring, Robert Rauschenberg and other contemporary artists.

▶ For fantastic Italian ice cream head to Caffé & Gelato in the Potsdamer Platz Arkaden (p67).

▶ From September to June, free classical concerts are held at 1pm Tuesday at the nearby Berliner Philharmonie (p67).

▶ For celeb-spotting, visit in February when Potsdamer Platz hosts the Berlinale film festival.

✗ Take a Break

Report to Qiu (p66) for sit-down lunches in stylish surroundings.

Short on time? Try the food-court-style eateries in the basement of the Potsdamer Platz Arkaden (p67).

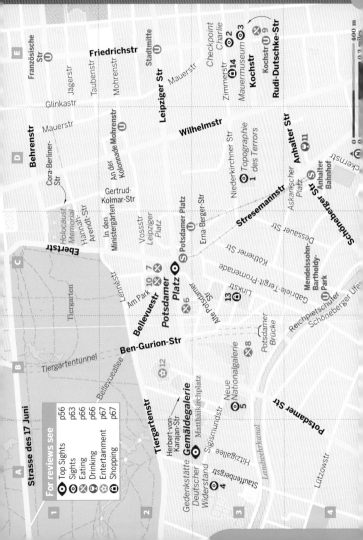

Strasse des 17 Juni

Tiergartentunnel

Tiergarten

Ebertstr

Holocaust Memorial

Cora-Berliner-Str

Behrenstr

Mauerstr

Franzosische Str

Jagerstr

Taubenstr

Mohrenstr

Friedrichstr

Stadtmitte

Glinkastr

Leipziger Str

Mauerstr

An der Kolonnade Mohrenstr

Gertrud-Kolmar-Str

Hannah-Arendt-Str

In den Ministergarten

Vossstr

Leipziger Platz

Wilhelmstr

Niederkirchner Str

Topographie des Terrors ⓵

Checkpoint Charlie

Zimmerstr

Mauermuseum ⓶ ⓷

⊗⓮

Kochstr

Kochstr ⓾ ⓽

Rudi-Dutschke-Str

Askanischer Platz

Anhalter Str

⊗⓫

Schoneberger Str

Anhalter Bahnhof

Stresemannstr

Dessauer Str

Potsdamer Platz Ⓢ

Erna-Berger-Str

Kothener Str

Gabriele-Tergit-Promenade

Reichpietschufer

Schoneberger Ufer

Mendelssohn-Bartholdy-Park

Eberstr

Lennestr

Am Park ⓾ ⓻⊗

Bellevuestr

Potsdamer Platz

⊗⓺

Linkstr

⓭

Alte Potsdamer Str

⊗⓼

Potsdamer Brucke

Ben-Gurion-Str

Bellevueallee

✪⓬

Tiergartenstr

Herbert-von-Karajan-Str

Gemaldegalerie

Matthaikirchplatz

Sigismundstr

Neue Nationalgalerie ⓾ ⓹

Potsdamer Str

Gedenkstatte Deutscher Widerstand

Stauffenbergstr

Hitzigallee

⊗⓸

Landwehrkanal

Lutzowstr

400 m
0.2 miles

Sights

Topographie des Terrors

MUSEUM

1 ⊙ Map p62, D3

In the same spot where once stood the most feared institutions of Nazi Germany (including the Gestapo headquarters and the SS central command), this excellent exhibit dissects the anatomy of the Nazi state by tracing the stages of terror and persecution, putting a face on the perpetrators and detailing the impact these brutal government departments had on all of Europe. (Topography of Terror; www.topographie.de; Niederkirchner Strasse 8; admission free; ◷10am-8pm; U-/S-Bahn Potsdamer Platz)

Checkpoint Charlie

LANDMARK

2 ⊙ Map p62, E3

Checkpoint Charlie was the principal gateway for Allies, other non-Germans and diplomats between the two Berlins from 1961 to 1990. Unfortunately, this potent symbol of the Cold War has become a tacky tourist trap where uniformed actors pose for tips in front of a replica guardhouse, although the free open-air exhibit chronicling Cold War history is one redeeming aspect. (cnr Friedrichstrasse & Zimmerstrasse; U-Bahn Kochstrasse)

Mauermuseum

MUSEUM

3 ⊙ Map p62, E3

The Cold War years, especially the history and horror of the Berlin Wall, are engagingly, if haphazardly, documented in this privately run tourist magnet. The best bits are about ingenious escapes to the West in hot-air balloons, tunnels, concealed car compartments and even a one-person submarine. (Berlin Wall Museum; www.mauermuseum.de; Friedrichstrasse 43-45; adult/concession €12.50/9.50; ◷9am-10pm; U-Bahn Kochstrasse)

☑ Top Tip

Kulturforum Museums

In addition to the Gemäldegalerie (p56) and the Neue Nationalgalerie (p64), the Kulturforum encompasses three other top-rated museums: the **Kupferstichkabinett** (Museum of Prints & Drawings; Map p62, B3; www.smb.museum; Matthäikirchplatz) with prints and drawings since the 14th century; the **Musikinstrumenten-Museum** (Musical Instrument Museum; Map p62, B2; www.sim.spk-berlin.de, in German; Tiergartenstrasse 1) with rare historical instruments; and the **Kunstgewerbemuseum** (Museum of Decorative Arts; Map p62, B2; www.smb.museum; Matthäikirchplatz), which is closed for renovation. A ticket to any Kulturforum museum entitles you to same-day admission to the permanent collections of any of the others.

Checkpoint Charlie (p63)

Gedenkstätte Deutscher Widerstand

MUSEUM

4 ⊙ Map p62, A3

This important exhibit on German Nazi resistance occupies the very rooms where high-ranking officers led by Claus Schenk Graf von Stauffenberg plotted the assassination attempt on Hitler on 20 July 1944. There's a memorial in the courtyard where the main conspirators were shot right after the failed coup, a story poignantly retold in the 2008 movie *Valkyrie*. (www.gdw-berlin.de; Stauffenbergstrasse 13-14; admission free; ⊙9am-6pm Mon-Wed & Fri, to 8pm Thu, 10am-6pm Sat & Sun; U-/S-Bahn Potsdamer Platz; 🚌M29)

Neue Nationalgalerie

GALLERY

5 ⊙ Map p62, B3

This light-flooded glass temple by Ludwig Mies van der Rohe presents international 20th-century art, including key works by Picasso, Max Beckmann and Gerhard Richter and an outstanding collection of German expressionists. (New National Gallery; www.smb.museum; Potsdamer Strasse 50; adult/concession €8/4; ⊙10am-6pm Tue-Wed & Fri-Sun, to 10pm Thu; U-/S-Bahn Potsdamer Platz; 🚌200, M29)

Understand

The Berlin Wall

It's more than a tad ironic that Berlin's most popular tourist attraction is one that no longer exists. For 28 years the Berlin Wall, the most potent symbol of the Cold War, divided not only a city but the world.

The Beginning

Shortly after midnight on 13 August 1961, East German soldiers and police began rolling out miles of barbed wire that would soon be replaced with prefabricated concrete slabs. The Wall was a desperate measure launched by the German Democratic Republic (GDR) government to stop the sustained brain and brawn drain the country had experienced since its 1949 founding. Some 3.6 million people had already headed to western Germany, putting the GDR on the brink of economic and political collapse.

The Physical Border

Euphemistically called the 'Anti-Fascist Protection Barrier', the Berlin Wall was continually reinforced and refined. In the end, it was a complex border-security system consisting of two walls hemming in a 'death strip' riddled with trenches, floodlights, attack dogs, electrified alarm fences and watchtowers staffed by guards with shoot-to-kill orders.

Nearly 100,000 GDR citizens tried to escape, many using spectacular contraptions like homemade hot-air balloons or U-boats. There are no exact numbers, but it is believed that hundreds died in the process.

The End

The Wall's demise came as unexpectedly as its creation. Once again the GDR was losing its people in droves, this time via Hungary, which had opened its borders with Austria. Major demonstrations in East Berlin culminated in early November 1989 when half a million people gathered on Alexanderplatz. Something had to give. It did on 9 November, when a GDR spokesperson mistakenly announced during a press conference on live TV that all travel restrictions to the West would be lifted. Immediately. Amid scenes of wild partying, the two Berlins came together again.

Today, only about 1.5km of the Berlin Wall still stands, while a double row of cobblestones embedded in the pavement traces its course.

Eating

Qiu

INTERNATIONAL €€

6 🍴 Map p62, C2

The two-course business lunch at this stylish lounge in the Mandala Hotel is a virtual steal. At night the sensuous setting amid mood-lit fringe lamps and golden mosaic waterfall is great for pre-dinner or post-show cocktails. (www.qiu.de; Mandala Hotel, Potsdamer Strasse 3; lunch €12; ⊙lunch Mon-Fri; U-/S-Bahn Potsdamer Platz; 🛜)

Vapiano

ITALIAN €

7 🍴 Map p62, C2

Matteo Thun's jazzy decor is a stylish foil for the tasty Italian fare at this successful German self-service chain. Mix-and-match pasta dishes, creative salads and crusty pizzas are prepared right before your eyes. Nice touch: tables with baskets of fresh basil and fragrant olive oil. (www.vapiano.de; Potsdamer Platz 5; mains €6-9; U-/S-Bahn Potsdamer Platz)

Weilands Wellfood

INTERNATIONAL €

8 🍴 Map p62, B3

The wholewheat pastas, vitamin-packed salads and fragrant wok dishes at this upbeat self-service bistro are perfect for health- and waist-watchers and best enjoyed outside by a little pond. (www.weilands-wellfood.de, in German; Marlene-Dietrich-Platz 1; mains €4-9; ⊙10am-10pm; U-/S-Bahn Potsdamer Platz; 🛜)

tazcafé

INTERNATIONAL €

9 🍴 Map p62, E3

Near Checkpoint Charlie, join *taz* newspaper staffers at fire-engine-red tables for daily-changing low-cost lunches with global pizzazz, and prepared with seasonal vegetables and free-range meats. Afternoons bring cakes, snacks and delicious fair-trade house espresso. (www.taz.de, in German; Rudi-Dutschke-Strasse 23; mains €6-7; ⊙8am-8pm Mon-Fri; U-Bahn Kochstrasse; 🛜)

Desbrosses

FRENCH €€€

10 🍴 Map p62, C2

The Ritz-Carlton's brasserie is anchored by an open kitchen with a race-car-red enamel oven and toqued chefs turning out upmarket French country classics – bouillabaisse, foie gras, *boeuf bourguignon*. Weekday lunch specials go for €14. (www.desbrosses.de; Ritz-Carlton, Potsdamer Platz 3; mains €16-39; ⊙breakfast, lunch & dinner; U-/S-Bahn Potsdamer Platz)

Drinking

Solar

BAR

11 🍷 Map p62, D4

Views of the Berlin skyline are truly impressive at this sparkling sky lounge hovering above an upscale dining room. With its dim lighting, the black leather sofas and swings make it a great spot for a date or sunset drinks. Even just getting there aboard

Interior of the Berliner Philharmonie

Scharoun's clever terraced vineyard design, not a bad seat in the house. It's the home base of the Berliner Philharmoniker, currently led by Sir Simon Rattle. Bonus: free Tuesday lunchtime concerts at 1pm, September to June. (☎2548 8999; www.berliner -philharmoniker.de; Herbert-von-Karajan- Strasse 1; U-/S-Bahn Potsdamer Platz)

Shopping

Potsdamer Platz Arkaden   MALL

13 🔒 Map p62, C3

You'll find all your basic shopping needs met at this attractive indoor mall. The basement has two super- markets and numerous fast-food outlets. (www.potsdamer-platz-arkaden.de; Alte Potsdamer Strasse; ⊙10am-9pm Mon- Sat; U-/S-Bahn Potsdamer Platz)

Frau Tonis Parfum   PERFUME

14 🔒 Map p62, E3

Follow your nose to this scent-sational made-in-Berlin perfume boutique. Try Marlene Dietrich's favourite (a bold violet) or ask for a customised fragrance. (www.frau-tonis-parfum.com; Zimmerstrasse 13; ⊙10am-6pm Mon-Sat; U-Bahn Kochstrasse)

an exterior glass lift is half the fun – at least if you're not vertigo-prone. It's behind the Pit Stop auto shop. (www .solar-berlin.de; Stresemannstrasse 76; S-Bahn Anhalter Bahnhof)

Entertainment

Berliner Philharmonie   CLASSICAL MUSIC

12 ⭐ Map p62, B2

This world-famous concert hall has supreme acoustics and, thanks to Hans

Top Sights
Jüdisches Museum

Getting There

The museum is about 1km south of Checkpoint Charlie.

U-Bahn From Kochstrasse station (U6) walk east on Kochstrasse, turn right on Markgrafenstrasse and right again on Lindenstrasse.

In a landmark building by American-Polish architect Daniel Libeskind, Berlin's Jewish Museum offers a chronicle of trials and triumphs in 2000 years of German-Jewish history. The exhibit smoothly navigates through all major periods, from the Romans and the Middle Ages to the Age of Enlightenment and the community's renaissance today. Find out about Jewish cultural contributions, holiday traditions, the difficult road to emancipation and outstanding individuals such as philosopher Moses Mendelssohn, jeans inventor Levi Strauss and painter Felix Nussbaum.

Don't Miss

The Building

Daniel Libeskind's stunning structure is essentially a 3D metaphor for the tortured history of the Jewish people. Its zigzag outline symbolises a broken Star of David; its silvery zinc walls are sharply angled; and instead of windows there are only small gashes piercing the gleaming facade.

Axes

The visual allegory continues inside, where a steep staircase descends to three intersecting walkways – called 'axes' – representing the fates of Jews during the Nazi years: death, exile and continuity. Only the latter leads to the exhibit.

Schalechet (Fallen Leaves)

Menashe Kadishman's art installation is one of the museum's most poignant. More than 10,000 open-mouthed faces cut from rusty iron plates lie scattered on the floor in an ocean of silent screams. The space itself, a claustrophobic cement-walled enclosure that Libeskind calls a Memory Void, is a metaphor for the loss of the murdered Jews of Europe.

Moses Mendelssohn Exhibit

Philosopher Moses Mendelssohn (1729–86) was a key figure in the Jewish Enlightenment. His progressive thinking and lobbying paved the way for the Emancipation Edict of 1812, which made Jews full Prussian citizens with equal rights.

Max Liebermann Self-Portrait

Max Liebermann (1847–1935) was Germany's most famous impressionist and co-founder of the Berlin Secession movement. This painting shows the Jewish artist as an old man in 1929, wearing his signature panama hat.

☑ 2599 3300

www.jmberlin.de

Lindenstrasse 9-14

adult/concession €5/2.50

🕙 10am-10pm Mon, to 8pm Tue-Sun

☑ Top Tips

▶ Rent the audioguide (€3) for an in-depth experience.

▶ Admission includes reduced entry on the same and following two days to the **Berlinische Galerie** (www.berlinische galerie.de; Alte Jakobstrasse 124; adult/concession €6/3; 🕙 10am-6pm Wed-Mon), an excellent survey of 100 years of Berlin art, just 500m away.

✕ Take a Break

The on-site **cafe** (mains €5-15) provides all-day sustenance in the glass courtyard and garden.

Head to edgily designed **Cafe Dix** (mains €5-10; 🕙 10am-7pm Wed-Mon) in the Berlinische Galerie for snacks, meals and cake.

Local Life
An Afternoon in the Bergmannkiez

Getting There

The Bergmannkiez is in the western part of Kreuzberg.

U-Bahn To start the itinerary, get off at Gneisenaustrasse (U7). When you're done, Mehringdamm station (U7) is closest.

One of Berlin's most charismatic neighbourhoods, the Bergmannkiez in gentrified western Kreuzberg is named for its main shopping strip, the Berg-mannstrasse, which is chock-a-block with people-watching cafes and quirky shops. Nearby, the decommissioned Tempelhof airport saw its finest hour during the 1948 Berlin Blockade. Above it all 'soars' the Kreuzberg hill, Berlin's highest natural elevation and a wonderful summertime play zone.

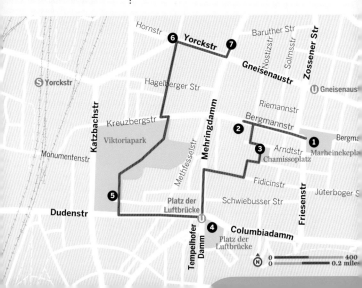

❶ Marheineke Markthalle

Thanks to a substantial renovation, the historic **Marheineke Market Hall** (www.meine-markthalle.de; Marheinekeplatz; ⏱8am-8pm Mon-Fri, to 6pm Sat) has traded its grungy 19th-century charm for bright and modern digs. Its aisles now brim with vendors plying everything from organic sausages to handmade cheeses, artisanal honey and other delicious bounty.

❷ Neubau

For a delicious sit-down meal, make a beeline for **Neubau** (www.neubau-restaurant.de; Bergmannstrasse 5; 2-course lunch €10, 3-course dinner €28; ⏱lunch & dinner Mon-Sat), where classic German comfort food gets a progressive twist that goes well with the airy, modern dining room.

❸ Chamissoplatz

On Saturday mornings the entire neighbourhood turns out for Berlin's longest-running organic farmers market held on pretty Chamissoplatz, framed by stately 19th-century townhouses. With cobbled streets, old-timey lanterns and even an octagonal *pissoir,* the entire square looks virtually unchanged a century on.

❹ Luftbrückendenkmal

The Airlift Memorial outside the former Tempelhof airport honours those who participated in keeping the city fed and free during the 1948 Berlin Blockade. The trio of spikes represents the three air corridors used by the Western Allies, while the plinth bears the names of the 79 people who died in this colossal effort.

❺ Viktoriapark

Take a break in this rambling park draped over the 66m-high Kreuzberg hill, home to a vineyard, a waterfall and a pompous memorial commemorating Napoleon's 1815 defeat. In summer, laid-back locals arrive to chill, tan or enjoy beers at **Golgatha** (www.golgatha-berlin.de, in German; Dudenstrasse 48-64; ⏱from 10am Apr-Sep), the park's classic beer garden.

❻ Yorckschlösschen

Cosy and knick-knack-laden, **Yorckschlösschen** (www.yorckschloesschen.de; Yorckstrasse 15; ⏱from 5pm Mon-Sat, 10am Sun; 🛜) is a Kreuzberg institution that has plied an all-ages, all-comers crowd of jazz and blues lovers with tunes and booze for over a century. There's live music several times weekly, cold beer on tap and German comfort food till 1am.

❼ Curry 36

Day after day, night after night, a motley crowd of tattooed scenesters, 'tie'd-up' office jockeys, noisy schoolkids and savvy tourists wait their turn at **Curry 36** (Mehringdamm 36; sausages around €2; ⏱9am-5am). Considered one of the top Currywurst purveyors in town, this once-humble-gone-high-tech stand has been frying 'em up since the days when Madonna was singing about virgins.

Explore

Scheunenviertel & Around

The Scheunenviertel (Barn Quarter) is one of Berlin's oldest, most charismatic neighbourhoods. Embark on an aimless wander and you'll constantly stumble upon enchanting surprises: here an idyllic courtyard or bleeding-edge gallery, there a fashion-forward boutique or belle époque ballroom. Since reunification, the Scheunenviertel has also reprised its historic role as Berlin's main Jewish Quarter.

The Sights in a Day

☀ Make your way to Nordbahnhof S-Bahn station to start the day with an in-depth study of the Berlin Wall at the **Gedenkstätte Berliner Mauer** (p74). Follow Bernauer Strasse east, then either walk down up-and-coming Brunnenstrasse, past galleries and shops, or hop on the U8 for the one-stop ride to Rosenthaler Platz and lunch at **Chén Chè** (p80).

☼ Spend the afternoon getting lost in the Scheunenviertel and stocking up on Berlin fashions and accessories in boutiques in the **Hackesche Höfe** (pictured left; p79) and along Alte Schönhauser Strasse, Neue Schönhauser Strasse, Münzstrasse, Rosenthaler Strasse and their side streets. Get your art fix at **KW Institute for Contemporary Art** (p79) and follow up with a strong cuppa in its courtyard Café Bravo. Interested in Berlin's Jewish community? Swing by the **Neue Synagoge** (p79) and the **Alter Jüdischer Friedhof** (p80).

☾ Report for dinner at **Schwarzwaldstuben** (p81) if you fancy rib-sticking southern German fare or at **Hartweizen** (p80) for superior Italian. Grab a digestive at **Neue Odessa Bar** (p83), then make your 'Astaire way to heaven' on the dance floor at the endearingly retro **Clärchens Ballhaus** (p82).

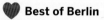 **Top Sights**

Gedenkstätte Berliner Mauer (p74)

💜 **Best of Berlin**

Eating
Chén Chè (p80)

Hartweizen (p80)

Kopps (p81)

Dolores (p81)

Bars
Neue Odessa Bar (p83)

Trust (p83)

KingSize Bar (p83)

Getting There

🚌 **Bus** The 142 runs along Torstrasse.

S-Bahn Hackescher Markt station (S5, S7, S9) puts you in the thick of the Scheunenviertel. Oranienburger Strasse (S1, S2) is another good jumping-off point.

🚊 **Tram** Number 1 makes stops at key spots within the quarter.

U-Bahn Weinmeisterstrasse (U8) is the most central station. Rosenthaler Platz (U8) and Rosa-Luxemburg-Platz (U2) are closer to Torstrasse and the northern Scheunenviertel.

Top Sights
Gedenkstätte Berliner Mauer

Stretching along Bernauer Strasse between Gartenstrasse and Ackerstrasse, the Berlin Wall Memorial is the central memorial site of German division. This is the only place where you can see how all the elements of the Wall and the 'death strip' fit together and learn how the border was enlarged and perfected over time (see p65). The indoor-outdoor installation vividly illustrates the role of the Wall in solidifying the GDR government's power. Several famous escape attempts took place along Bernauer Strasse.

👁 Map p76, C1

www.berliner-mauer
-gedenkstaette.de

Bernauer Strasse 119

admission free

🕙exhibit 9.30am-6pm
or 7pm Tue-Sun, outdoor
installations 8am-10pm

S-Bahn Nordbahnhof

Don't Miss

National Monument

Honouring the memory of Berlin Wall victims is a 70m section of original wall bounded by two rusted steel flanks. Beyond is a reconstructed 'death strip' complete with a sandy path once patrolled by motorised guards, the lamps that bathed it in fierce light at night, and a guard tower.

Berliner Mauer Dokumentationszentrum

For a sweeping overview of the monument and adjacent grounds, climb to the viewing platform of the Berlin Wall Documentation Center. Inside, a small exhibit uses photographs, recordings and archival documents to detail the events leading up to that fateful day in August 1961 when the first spools of barbed wire were unrolled.

Kapelle der Versöhnung

The simple but radiant Chapel of Reconciliation stands on the foundations of a 19th-century church that wound up in the middle of the 'death strip' and was blown up in 1985.

Window of Remembrance

A wall of portraits gives identity to the people who lost their lives at the Berlin Wall. The park-like area surrounding the installation was once part of the adjacent cemetery; more than 1000 graves were relocated to make room for the Wall.

Nordbahnhof 'Ghost Station'

The Wall also divided the city's transportation system. Three lines with stations in West Berlin used tracks that ran through the eastern sector to return to stations on the western side. Stations on East Berlin turf were closed and patrolled by GDR guards. Nordbahnhof, one of these so-called 'ghost stations', has an on-site exhibit.

☑ Top Tips

▶ The visitor centre screens a short introductory film and hands out free maps of the memorial grounds.

▶ A 15-minute remembrance service for the Wall victims is held in the Chapel of Reconciliation at noon Tuesday to Friday.

✗ Take a Break

The closest cafe to the memorial is the **Mauercafe** (Map p76, C1; www .mauercafe-berlin.de; Bernauer Strasse 117), which does breakfast, snacks, coffee and ice creams.

Right at Bernauer Strasse U-Bahn station, **Cafe Grenzenlos** (Map p76, E1; Brunnenstrasse 47) is another good bet for coffee, cakes and breakfast.

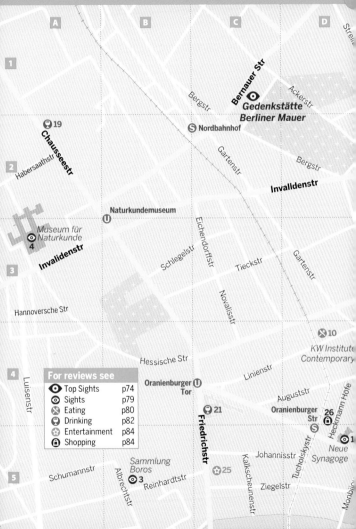

A

B

C

D

1

Bernauer Str

Ackerstr

Gedenkstätte
Berliner Mauer

Bergstr

S Nordbahnhof

19

Chausseestr

Bergstr

Gartenstr

2

Habersaathstr

Invalidenstr

Naturkundemuseum
U

Eichendorffstr

Gartenstr

Museum für
Naturkunde
4

Schlegelstr

Tieckstr

3

Invalidenstr

Novalisstr

Hannoversche Str

10

KW Institute
Contemporary

4

Hessische Str

Linienstr

Luisenstr

For reviews see

⦿ Top Sights   p74
⦿ Sights   p79
✕ Eating   p80
⦿ Drinking   p82
✪ Entertainment   p84
🔒 Shopping   p84

Oranienburger U
Tor

Auguststr

Oranienburger
Str S

Heckmann Höfe

26

21

Friedrichstr

Johannisstr

1

Neue
Synagogue

Schumannstr

Sammlung
Boros
3

Albrechtstr

Reinhardtstr

25

Kalkscheunenstr

Tucholskystr

Ziegelstr

Monbijou

E   **F**   **G**   **H**

Ruppinerstr

0   400 m
0   0.2 miles

Schönhauser Allee

1

Anklamer Str

Fehrbelliner Str

Zionskirchplatz

Brunnenstr

Kastanienallee

Schwedter Str

Veteranenstr

Choriner Str

2

Volkspark am
Weinbergsweg

Weinbergsweg

Senefelderplatz Ⓤ

Teutoburger
Platz

Schönhauser Allee

Rosenthaler
Platz
17 Ⓤ

18

3

Torstr

Rosenthaler Str

Torstr

14

13 ✕

Linienstr

✕ 7

22

20

Koppenplatz

Linienstr

Auguststr

12

Ⓤ Rosa-
Luxemburg-
Platz

◑16

Grosse Hamburger Str

Gipsstr

8
24

Gormannstr

Mulackstr

4

✕ 15 Sophie-Gips-
Höfe

Sophienstr

Steinstr

Alte Schönhauser Str

Max-Beer-Str

Almstadtstr

Hirtenstr

Weydinger Str

ausnickstr

27 🔒

Hackesche
Höfe

28 Ⓤ Weinmeisterstr

9

Rosa-Luxemburg-Str

Prenzlauer Allee

Alter
Jüdischer
Friedhof

6

2

Neue Schönhauser Str

Münzstr

29
Memhardstr

5

anienburger Str

Monbijouplatz

Monbijou
Park

Dircksenstr

11

Understand

Jewish Berlin

Since reunification, Berlin has had the fastest-growing Jewish community in the world. Its background is diverse; most are Russian Jewish immigrants but there are also Jews of German heritage, Israelis wishing to escape their politically frustrating homeland and American expats lured by Berlin's low-cost living and limitless creativity. Today there are about 13,000 active members of the Jewish community, including 1000 belonging to the Orthodox congregation Adass Yisroel. However, since not all Jews choose to be affiliated with a synagogue, the actual population is estimated to be at least twice as high.

Community Roots

Records show that Jews first settled in Berlin in 1295, but throughout the Middle Ages they had to contend with being blamed for any kind of societal or economic woe. When the plague struck (1348–49), rumours that Jews had poisoned the wells led to the first major pogrom. In 1510, 38 Jews were publicly tortured and burned for allegedly stealing the host from a church because a confession by the actual (Christian) perpetrator was deemed too straightforward to be true.

Financial interests, not humanitarian ones, motivated the Elector Friedrich Wilhelm to invite Jewish families expelled from Vienna to settle in Berlin in 1671. To his credit, he later extended the offer to Jews in general and also allowed them to practise their faith – which at the time was still considered a privilege throughout Europe.

The Last Century

By the late 19th century, many of Berlin's Jews, numbering about 5% of the city population, had become thoroughly German in speech and identity. When a wave of Hasidic Jews escaping the pogroms of Eastern Europe arrived around the same time, they found their way to today's Scheunenviertel, which at that time was an immigrant slum with cheap housing. By 1933 Berlin's Jewish population had grown to around 160,000 and constituted one-third of all Jews living in Germany. The well-known horrors of the Nazi years sent most into exile and left 55,000 dead. Only 1000 to 2000 Jews are believed to have survived the war years in Berlin, often with the help of their non-Jewish neighbours.

Sights

Neue Synagoge
SYNAGOGUE

1 ⊙ Map p76, D5

The gilded dome of the New Synagogue is the most visible symbol of Berlin's revitalised Jewish community. The 1866 original was Germany's largest synagogue but its modern incarnation is not so much a house of worship as a place of remembrance called Centrum Judaicum. Climb the dome to gaze out over the Scheunenviertel's rooftops. (www.cjudaicum.de; Oranienburger Strasse 28-30; adult/concession €3/2; ⊙10am-8pm Sun & Mon, to 6pm Tue-Thu, to 5pm Fri Apr-Sep, 10am-8pm Sun & Mon, to 6pm Tue-Thu, to 2pm Fri Oct & Mar, 10am-6pm Sun-Thu, to 2pm Fri Nov-Feb; S-Bahn Oranienburger Strasse; 🚃M1)

Hackesche Höfe
HISTORIC SITE

2 ⊙ Map p76, F5

The Hackesche Höfe is the largest and most famous of the restored courtyard ensembles peppering the Scheunenviertel. Take your time pottering around the cafes, old-fashioned variety theatre, art-house cinema and high-end local-designer stores. Enter from Rosenthaler Strasse or Sophienstrasse. (www.hackesche-hoefe.com, in German; S-Bahn Hackescher Markt; 🚃M1)

Sammlung Boros
GALLERY

3 ⊙ Map p76, B5

The vibe of war still hangs over this Nazi-era bunker turned shining beacon of art thanks to a stellar private collection of artists currently writing history – Olafur Eliasson, Damien Hirst, Sarah Lucas and Wolfgang Tillmans among them. Entry is by guided tour (also in English) only; book online as early as possible. (Boros Collection; www.sammlung-boros.de; Reinhardtstrasse 20; tours €10; ⊙Fri, Sat & Sun; U-Bahn Oranienburger Tor; U-/S-Bahn Friedrichstrasse)

Museum für Naturkunde
MUSEUM

4 ⊙ Map p76, A3

Fossils and minerals don't quicken your pulse? Well, how about a 23m-long and 12m-high brachiosaurus, the world's largest mounted dino? The giant lizard is joined by a dozen other Jurassic buddies, an ultra-rare archaeopteryx and, soon, the world's most famous dead polar bear, Knut. (Museum of Natural History; www.naturkundemuseum-berlin.de; Invalidenstrasse 43; adult/concession €6/3.50; ⊙9.30am-6pm Tue-Fri, 10am-6pm Sat & Sun; U-Bahn Naturkundemuseum)

KW Institute for Contemporary Art
GALLERY

5 ⊙ Map p76, D4

In an old margarine factory, KW stages shows reflecting the latest – and often radical – trends in contemporary art. Café Bravo in the courtyard makes for a suitably artistic coffee break. (www.kw-berlin.de; Auguststrasse 69; adult/concession €6/4; ⊙noon-7pm Tue, Wed & Fri-Sun, to 9pm Thu; S-Bahn Oranienburger Strasse; 🚃M1)

Alter Jüdischer Friedhof
CEMETERY

6 Map p76, E5

Berlin's first Jewish cemetery was destroyed by the Gestapo in 1943. A replica of Enlightenment philosopher Moses Mendelssohn's tombstone stands as a lone representative for all 6ft-under residents buried here between 1672 and 1827. (Old Jewish Cemetery; Grosse Hamburger Strasse; S-Bahn Hackescher Markt; M1)

Eating

Hartweizen
ITALIAN €€

7 Map p76, F3

With its simple wooden tables, panorama windows and bright bulbs, Hartweizen is aeons away from Chianti-bottle kitsch but, quite simply, a top Italian restaurant focused on the flavours of the Puglia region. Fish and meat are first-rate, the pastas home-made, portions plentiful and even the cheapest bottle of wine (€17) a satisfying drop. (2849 3877; www.hartweizen.com; Torstrasse 96; mains €10-18; dinner Mon-Sat; U-Bahn Rosenthaler Platz; M1)

Chén Chè
VIETNAMESE €€

8 Map p76, F4

Smouldering joss sticks point the way to this courtyard Vietnamese teahouse. Settle down in the charming Zen garden or beneath the huge hexagonal chandelier and tuck into traditional clay pots filled with steaming *pho* (soups), curries or noodle dishes. (www.chenche-berlin.de; Rosenthaler Strasse 13; mains €6.50-9; U-Bahn Rosenthaler Platz;)

Susuru
JAPANESE €

9 Map p76, H5

Go ye forth and slurp! Susuru is Japanese for 'slurping' and, quite frankly, that's really the best way to deal with the oodles of noodles at this soup parlour, which looks as neat and stylish

---

Understand
Scheunenviertel: From Hay to Hip

The Scheunenviertel's odd name (Barn Quarter) hearkens back centuries to the days of wooden houses, frequent fires and poor fire-fighting techniques, which is why the Prussian king ordered all barns containing flammable crops to be stored outside the city walls. In the early 20th century, the quarter absorbed huge numbers of poor Eastern European Jewish immigrants, many of whom were annihilated by the Nazis. After the war the Scheunenviertel gradually deteriorated into a down-at-heel East Berlin quarter, but it has catapulted from drab to fab since reunification. Now a creative-class darling, its cafes and bars brim with iPad-toters, sassy fashionistas and skinny stray artists.

as a bento box. (www.susuru.de, in German; Rosa-Luxemburg-Strasse 17; soups €6.50-9; U-Bahn Rosa-Luxemburg-Platz; 📶 🌿)

Schwarzwaldstuben
GERMAN **€€**

10 Map p76, D4

In the mood for a Hansel and Gretel moment? Then join the other 'lost kids' in this send-up of the Black Forest complete with plastic pines and baseball-capped Bambi heads. We can't get enough of the *geschmelzte Maultaschen* (sautéed ravioli-like pasta) and the giant schnitzel. (☎2809 8084; Tucholskystrasse 48; mains €7-14; 🕘9am-midnight; S-Bahn Oranienburger Strasse; 🚋M1)

Dolores
CALIFORNIAN **€**

11 Map p76, H5

This is a bastion of California-style burritos – fresh, authentic and priced to help you stay on budget. Select your preferred combo of marinated meats or tofu, beans, veggies, salsa and cheese and the cheerful staff will build it on the spot. (www.dolores-berlin.de, in German; Rosa-Luxemburg-Strasse 7; burritos €4-6; 🕘11.30am-10pm Mon-Sat, from 1pm Sun; U-Bahn Weinmeisterstrasse, Alexanderplatz; 🌿)

Yam Yam
KOREAN **€**

12 Map p76, H4

In a dashing move of career derring-do, Sumi Ha morphed her fancy fashion boutique into a stylish self-service gem where the spicy *bibimbap* (a hot-pot rice dish), fresh *gimbab* (seaweed rolls), steamy *mandu* (dumplings) and other fancified Korean street food all

Art at Kunsthaus Tacheles, Oranienburger Strasse

pass the authenticity test. (www.yamyam-berlin.de; dishes €4.50-8; Alte Schönhauser Strasse 6; U-Bahn Rosenthaler Platz; 🚋M1)

Kopps
VEGAN **€€**

13 Map p76, E3

'Vegan German food' may seem like an oxymoron but not at Kopps, which dishes up delicious goulash, *rouladen* (beef olives) and schnitzel without using a single animal product. The space is sparse but stylish, with grey-blue walls and recycled doors and mirrors in unexpected places. Excellent breakfasts and bursting weekend brunch. (☎4320 9775; www.kopps-berlin.de; Linienstrasse 94; mains €9-14; 🕘8.30am-midnight; U-Bahn Rosenthaler Platz; 🚋M1; 🌿)

White Trash Fast Food AMERICAN €€

14  Map p76, H3

Wally Potts – city cowboy, California import and Berlin's coolest bar owner – has spun this ex-Irish pub into a borderline insane culinary punkhole. DJs or live bands make conversation a challenge, thus inadvertently helping you focus on the manly burgers and steaks flown straight in from the US of A. (☎5034 8668; www.whitetrashfastfood.com; Schönhauser Allee 6-7; mains €7.50-20; ☉lunch Mon-Fri, dinner daily; U-Bahn Rosa-Luxemburg-Platz)

Barcomi's Deli AMERICAN €

15  Map p76, F4

Join latte-rati, families and expats in this quiet courtyard cafe for custom-roasted coffee, wraps, bagels with lox, and possibly the best brownies and cheesecake this side of the Hudson

Doner kebab vendor on Rosenthaler Platz

River. (www.barcomis.de, in German; 2nd courtyard, Sophie-Gips-Höfe, Sophienstrasse 21; dishes €3-12; ☉9am-9pm Mon-Sat, 10am-9pm Sun; U-Bahn Weinmeisterstrasse; ☒)

◯ Local Life
Rosenthaler Platz: Snack Central

For feeding hunger pangs on the quick and cheap, choices could not be greater than around Rosenthaler Platz U-Bahn station (Map p76, F3). Our three faves are **Grill- und Schlemmerbuffet** (Torstrasse 125) for Oscar-worthy doner kebabs, **Rosenburger** (Brunnenstrasse 196) for freshly made burgers, and **CôCô** (Rosenthaler Strasse 2) for bulging *banh mi* (Vietnamese sandwiches).

Drinking

Clärchens Ballhaus

CLUB, RESTAURANT

16  Map p76, E4

Yesteryear is now at this late, great 19th-century dance hall, where groovers and grannies hoof it across the wooden floor without an ounce of irony. There are different sounds nightly (salsa, swing, tango, disco) and a live band on Saturdays. Pizza and German staples provide sustenance, in summer in the pretty garden. (www

.ballhaus-mitte.de, in German; Auguststrasse 24; ⊙from 10pm Mon, 9pm Tue-Thu, 8pm Fri & Sat, 3pm Sun; S-Bahn Oranienburger Strasse)

Mein Haus am See
CAFE, BAR

17 🚇 Map p76, F3

The terraced steps make for the perfect people-watching perch in this chill cafe-bar, which gets street cred from readings, concerts, DJs and other cultural events. (www.mein-haus-am-see .blogspot.com; Brunnenstrasse 197/198; ⊙from 9am; U-Bahn Rosenthaler Platz)

Neue Odessa Bar
BAR

18 🚇 Map p76, G3

Rub shoulders with a global mix of grown-ups with a hot fashion sense at this comfy-chic and always busy Torstrasse staple. The patterned wallpaper, velvet sofas and smart lamps create cosy ambience, no matter if your taste runs toward Krusovice or cocktails. Smoking allowed. (www .neueodessabar.de; Torstrasse 89; ⊙from 7pm; U-Bahn Rosenthaler Platz)

K-TV
CLUB

19 🚇 Map p76, A2

Behind a graffiti-festooned facade across from the new BND building (ie the German CIA) awaits this cavernous club whose improvised grit recalls the '90s, even if the long-drink-guzzling and champagne-swilling patrons are very 2010s. Bar on ground floor; electro in the basement. Smoking allowed. (www.ktv-berlin.de; Chausseestrasse 36; ⊙Fri & Sat; U-Bahn Naturkundemuseum)

Kaffee Burger
BAR, CLUB

20 🚇 Map p76, H3

This sweaty club with lovingly faded East German decor is the famous home of the twice-monthly Russendisko (Russian Disco) that even Madonna couldn't resist. But even without a tabloid-regular in sight, it's always a fun-for-all party pen with almost-nightly concerts (indie, punk, rock, Balkanbeats), plus Sunday readings. (www.kaffeeburger.de; Torstrasse 58/60; ⊙from 8pm Mon-Sat, 7pm Sun; U-Bahn Rosa-Luxemburg-Platz)

KingSize Bar
BAR

21 🚇 Map p76, C4

Delightfully self-ironic, this former GDR-era gay dive has about the dimensions of a large shoebox. Once you've 'shoehorned' your way past the door, it's a great place to get the evening started – or faded – by swilling your crystal whisky tumbler. Smoking allowed. (www .kingsizebar.de; Friedrichstrasse 112b; ⊙Wed-Sat; U-Bahn Oranienburger Tor; 🚊M1)

Trust
BAR

22 🚇 Map p76, G3

A Midas-touch venture by the club impresarios of Cookies (p37) and Weekend (p53), this golden-hued, trashy-chic bar is a buzzy pre-clubbing launch pad. Booze is sold only by the bottle to encourage sharing and thus 'trusting' your fellow drinkers. The concept carries over to the toilets. How? See for yourself, provided you make it past the doorstaff. Smoking

Q Local Life
Trendy Torstrasse

Though loud, ho-hum and heavily trafficked, Torstrasse is booming, and not just since Brangelina were rumoured to have bought a flat nearby. With surprising speed it has turned into a funky-town strip where trendy new eateries pop up all the time, gritty-glam bars pack in night crawlers and indie boutiques lure the fashion-savvy. The most happening section is between Schönhauser Allee and Rosenthaler Strasse.

allowed. (Torstrasse 72; ⏲from 10pm Thu-Sat; U-Bahn Rosenthaler Platz, Rosa-Luxemburg-Platz)

Entertainment

Chamäleon Varieté   CABARET

23 ⭐ Map p76, F5

A marriage of art nouveau charms and high-tech theatre trappings, this intimate 1920s-style cabaret in an old ballroom presents classy variety shows – comedy, juggling acts and singing – often in sassy, sexy and unconventional fashion. (☎400 0590; www.chamaeleonberlin.de, in German; Hackesche Höfe, Rosenthaler Strasse 40/41; S-Bahn Hackescher Markt)

B-Flat   LIVE MUSIC

24 ⭐ Map p76, F4

Cool cats of all ages come out to this intimate venue, where you'll sit quite literally within spitting distance of the performers. The emphasis is on acoustic music, mostly jazz, world beats, Afro-Brazilian and other soundscapes. Wednesday's free jam session often brings down the house. (☎283 3123; www.b-flat-berlin.de; Rosenthaler Strasse 13; ⏲from 8pm Sun-Thu, 9pm Fri-Sat; U-Bahn Weinmeisterstrasse)

Friedrichstadtpalast   CABARET

25 ⭐ Map p76, C5

Europe's largest revue theatre is famous for glitzy-glam Vegas-style productions with leggy showgirls, a high-tech stage, mindboggling special effects and plenty of artistry. (☎2326 2326; www.show-palace.eu; Friedrichstrasse 107; U-/S-Bahn Friedrichstrasse)

Shopping

Bonbonmacherei   FOOD

26 🔒 Map p76, D4

The aroma of peppermint and liquorice fills this old-fashioned basement candy kitchen, whose owners use antique equipment and time-tested recipes to churn out such tasty treats as Berliner Maiblätter (May leaves, made with woodruff). (www.bonbonmacherei.de, in German; Oranienburger Strasse 32, Heckmannhöfe; ⏲noon-8pm Wed-Sat, closed Jul & Aug; S-Bahn Oranienburger Strasse)

Ampelmann Galerie GIFTS, SOUVENIRS

27 🔒 Map p76, F5

It took a vociferous grass-roots campaign to save the little Ampelmann, the endearing fellow on East German pedestrian traffic lights. Now the beloved cult figure graces an entire store's worth of T-shirts, towels, key rings, cookie cutters and other knick-knacks. (www.ampelmann.de; Court V, Hackesche Höfe; ⏱9.30am-10pm Mon-Sat, 10am-7pm Sun; S-Bahn Hackescher Markt)

1. Absinth Depot Berlin DRINK

28 🔒 Map p76, G5

Van Gogh, Toulouse-Lautrec and Oscar Wilde were among the fin-de-siècle artists who drew, ahem, inspiration from the 'green fairy', as absinthe is also known. Ask this quaint shop's owner to help you pick out the perfect bottle for your own mind-altering rendezvous. (www.erstesabsinthdepotberlin.de; Weinmeisterstrasse 4; ⏱2pm-midnight Mon-Fri, from 1pm Sat; U-Bahn Weinmeisterstrasse)

Apartment FASHION

29 🔒 Map p76, H5

A staircase spirals down to one of Berlin's best-edited his-and-her concept stores. Once inside the plush jet-black boutique, sift through clothes by Palais Royal, Rich Owens, Tuesday Night Band Practice, Cheap Monday and other fashion-forward labels. (www.apartmentberlin.de; Memhardstrasse 8; ⏱11am-7pm Mon-Fri, noon-7pm Sat; U-Bahn Weinmeisterstrasse)

Ampelmann trinkets at Ampelmann Galerie

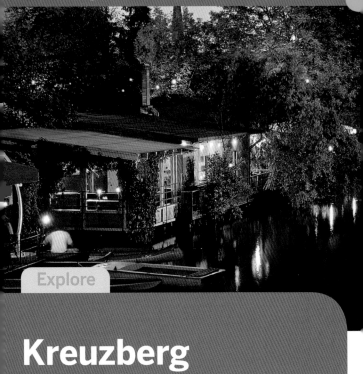

Explore

Kreuzberg

Creeping gentrification aside, Kreuzberg is still Berlin's hippest quarter, a bubbly hodgepodge of tousled students, aspiring creatives, shisha-smoking Turks and a global swarm of neo-Berliners. Spend a day searching for street art, soaking up the multiculti vibe, scarfing a shwarma, browsing vintage stores and hanging by the canal, then find out why Kreuzberg is also known as a night-crawler's paradise.

The Sights in a Day

☀ If it's a warm and sunny summer day, there are few better places to start your Kreuzberg sojourn than with a few hours of tanning, swimming and chilling in the **Badeschiff** (p97), a riverside beach and swimming pool.

☀ Once you've had your relaxation fill, walk north on Schlesische Strasse, taking in the large-scale **street art** (p92) of Blu and the unique fashions at **Killerbeast** (p97). For lunch, join the queue at **Burgermeister** (p94), then hop on the U1 for the one-stop ride to Görlitzer Bahnhof (or walk on Skalitzer Strasse). Follow Oranien-strasse north, checking out **UKO Fashion** (p97) and other secondhand, streetwear and knick-knack shops. Study the local boho crowd over coffee (or the first beer of the day) at **Luzia** (p89).

☾ After dark is when Kreuzberg truly comes alive. Dinner options range from haute cuisine at **Horváth** (p92) to rib-sticking German classics at **Max und Moritz** (p94). The latter is probably a better choice if you're planning to make a dedicated study of Kreuzberg's bar scene. For further suggestions see p94 and our Kotti Bar-Hop feature on p88.

🔍 **Local Life**

Kotti Bar-Hop (p88)

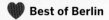 **Best of Berlin**

Eating
Burgermeister (p94)

Max und Moritz (p94)

Horváth (p92)

Defne (p92)

Bars
Würgeengel (p89)

Freischwimmer (pictured left; p96)

Club der Visionäre (p94)

Monarch Bar (p88)

Madame Claude (p96)

Clubs
Watergate (p94)

Gay & Lesbian
Roses (p89)

Möbel Olfe (p89)

SO36 (p89)

Getting There

U-Bahn Getting off at Kottbusser Tor (U8) puts you in the thick of Kreuzberg, but Görlitzer Bahnhof and Schlesisches Tor (both U1) are also good jumping-off points.

Local Life
Kotti Bar-Hop

Noisy, chaotic and sleepless, the area around Kottbusser Tor U-Bahn station (Kotti, for short) defiantly retains the punky-funky alt feel that's defined it since the 1970s. More gritty than pretty, this beehive of snack shops, cafes, pubs and bars delivers some of the city's most hot-stepping night-time action and is tailor-made for dedicated bar-hopping.

❶ Monarch Bar

Behind a window front at eye level with the elevated U-Bahn tracks, **Monarch Bar** (www.kottimonarch.de; Skalitzer Strasse 134; ⊙from 9pm Tue-Sat) is an ingenious blend of trashy sophistication, strong drinks, a relaxed vibe and different DJs nightly playing bouncy electro. Enter via the signless steel door adjacent to the doner kebab shop east of the Kaiser's supermarket.

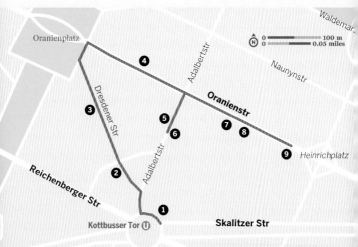

2 Möbel Olfe

An old furniture store, **Möbel Olfe** (www.moebel-olfe.de, in German; Reichenberger Strasse 177; Tue-Sun) has been recast as an always-busy drinking den with cheap libations and a friendly crowd that's mixed in every respect (gays dominate on Thursdays). Watch out: the skeletons above the bar get downright trippy after a few Polish beers or vodkas. Enter from Dresdener Strasse. Smoking OK.

3 Würgeengel

For a swish night out, point the compass to **Würgeengel** (www.wuergeengel.de, in German; Dresdener Strasse 122), a stylish '50s cocktail cave complete with chandeliers and shiny black tables. It's always busy but especially so after the final credits roll at the adjacent Babylon cinema. Smoking allowed.

4 Luzia

Tarted up nicely with vintage furniture, baroque wallpaper and whimsical wall art by Chin Chin, **Luzia** (Oranienstrasse 34; from noon; 📶) draws its crowd from among more sophisticated local urban dwellers. Some punters have derided it as Mitte-goes-Kreuzberg but it's still a comfy spot with lighting that gives hipsters a glow. Smokers' lounge.

5 Maroush

A warm and woodsy hole-in-the-wall, **Maroush** (www.maroush-berlin.de, in German; Adalbertstrasse 93; sandwiches €3; 11am-2am) is tailor-made for restoring balance to the brain with terrific felafel or shwarma sandwiches.

6 Hasir

The mother branch of a local Turkish mini-chain, **Hasir** (www.hasir.de; Adalbertstrasse 12; mains €8-13; 24hr) is packed at all hours with patrons lusting after grilled meats, stuffed vine leaves and other tasty morsels. Owner Mehmed Aygün claims to have invented the Berlin-style doner kebab back in 1971.

7 Bierhimmel

A hetero-friendly gay hang-out, **Bierhimmel** (Oranienstrasse 183; 1pm-3am) gets the coffee-and-cake crowd but is also a relaxed place to get the evening into gear before moving on to saucier places like Roses.

8 Roses

Camp and kitsch, **Roses** (Oranienstrasse 187; from 9pm) is a glittery fixture on the Kreuzberg circuit. Drinks are cheap and generous, making it a packed – and polysexual – pit stop during nights on the razzle. Smoking OK.

9 SO36

The Dead Kennedys and Die Toten Hosen played gigs at **SO36** (www.so36.de; Oranienstrasse 190) when many of today's patrons were still in nappies (diapers). Who goes when depends on what's on that night: a 'solidarity' concert, a lesbigay theme party, a night flea market – anything goes at this long-time epicentre of Kreuzberg's scruffy alt scene.

A · B · C · D

1

Heinrich-
Heine-
Platz

Leuschnerdamm

Engeldamm
Bethaniendamm

Mariannenplatz

Manteuffelstr

Waldemarstr

Dresdener Str

Oranienstr
6

5

Oranienplatz

Muskauer Str

2

Dresdener Str

Oranienstr

Naunynstr

Adalbertstr

Reichenberger Str

Heinrichplatz

19

Görlitzer
Bahnhof

Wassertorplatz

Kottbusser
Tor

Skalitzer Str

Spreewaldp

7

KREUZBERG

3

Admiralstr

Marianneplatz

20

Manteuffelstr

Reichenberger Str

Lausitzer Str

Fraenkelufer

Ohlauer Str

Urbanhafen

Planufer

3

1

14

Paul-Lincke-Ufer

Landwehrkanal

2

9

Grimmstr

Kottbusser Damm

Maybachufer

4

Böckhstr

Schönleinstr

Bürknerstr

Dieffenbachstr

Sanderstr

Hobrechtstr

Friedelstr

KREUZKÖLLN

Fichtestr

Hohenstaufenplatz

Pflügerstr

5

Urbanstr

Nansi

For reviews see

Eating

Horváth
AUSTRIAN €€€

1 🍴 | Map p90, B4

At his canalside bistro, Sebastian Frank (newly minted Michelin chef in 2011) performs culinary alchemy with Austrian classics, fearlessly combining textures, flavours and ingredients. To truly test his talents, order the 10-course small-plate dinner (€73). (☎6128 9992; www.restaurant-horvath.de, in German; Paul-Lincke-Ufer 44a; 3-course dinner from €39; ☉6pm-1am Tue-Sun; U-Bahn Kottbusser Tor)

Volt
GERMAN €€€

2 🍴 | Map p90, D4

The theatrical setting in a 1928 transformer station would be enough reason to seek out the culinary outpost of Matthias Geiss, one of Berlin's most promising new chefs. More drama awaits on the plates, where regional meats, fish and vegetables put on an artful show in innovative honest-to-goodness ways. (☎6107 4033; www.restaurant-volt.de; Paul-Lincke-Ufer 21; 3-course dinner €34, mains €24-32; ☉dinner Mon-Sat; U-Bahn Kottbusser Tor)

Defne
TURKISH €€

3 🍴 | Map p90, B4

If you thought Turkish cuisine stopped at the doner kebab, Defne will teach you otherwise. Start with finger-licking hummus, garlicky carrot or walnut-chilli paste, then move on to such satisfying mains as *ali nazik* (lamb with pureed eggplant and yoghurt). The

---

Understand
Street Art

Stencils, paste-ups, throw-ups, burners, bombings, pieces, murals, installations and 3D graffiti are the magic words in street art, describing styles and techniques that have little to do with vandalism, tagging and illegal scrawls. With no shortage of vacant buildings and weedy lots, sometimes it seems as though all of Berlin has become a canvas. Some of the hottest international artists have left their mark on local walls, including Banksy, Os Gemeos, Romero, Swoon, Flix, Pure Evil, Miss Van and Blu. The latter is especially prevalent in Kreuzberg, where it took the Italian artist just five days to cover an entire firewall with a huge pink body consisting of hundreds of smaller bodies writhing like worms. Called **Blackjump Mural**, it's at Falckensteinstrasse 48, next to Watergate (p94). Around the corner, on Schlesische Strasse at Cuvrystrasse, another wall features Blu's **Floating Giants**, one upside down, and a tie-wearing man handcuffed to his watches. There's plenty more great art around town. Just keep your eyes open or join a guided tour (p160).

Street art by Blu on Schlesische Strasse at Cuvrystrasse

canalside location is idyllic, the decor warmly exotic and the service top-notch. (☎ 8179 7111; www.defne-restaurant .de; Planufer 92c; mains €7.50-16; ☉ dinner; U-Bahn Schönleinstrasse)

Bar Raval
SPANISH €€

4 🍴 Map p90, E3

Bye-bye folklore kitsch. This tapas bar is fit for the 21st century. The brain-child of Spanish-German actor Daniel Brühl, the focus here is squarely on Iberian morsels ranging from classic *patatas bravas* (crisp fried potato) with homemade aioli to *sobrasada* (a pâté-style sausage from Mallorca). Monday is paella night. (☎ 5316 7954; www.barraval.de; Lübbener Strasse 1; tapas from €4; ☉ dinner daily, lunch Sat & Sun; U-Bahn Görlitzer Bahnhof)

Henne
GERMAN €

5 🍴 Map p90, B2

This rustic Old Berlin institution operates on the 'KISS' (keep it simple, stupid!) principle: milk-fed chicken spun on the rotisserie for a tan as perfect as George Hamilton's. That's all they've been serving for a century or so, alongside tangy potato and white cabbage salads. Garden seating in summer. Reservations a must. (☎ 614 7730; www.henne-berlin.de, in German; Leuschnerdamm 25; half-chicken €7.90; ☉ from 7pm Tue-Sat, from 5pm Sun; U-Bahn Kottbusser Tor, Moritzplatz)

Max und Moritz
GERMAN €€

6 Map p90, A2

The patina of yesteryear hangs over this ode-to-old-school brewpub named for the cheeky Wilhelm Busch cartoon characters. Since 1902 it has packed hungry eaters into its rustic tile-and-stucco ornamented rooms for sudsy home brews and granny-style Berlin fare. (www.maxundmoritzberlin.de; Oranienstrasse 162; mains €9-15; ⏱from 5pm; U-Bahn Moritzplatz)

Kimchi Princess
KOREAN €€

7 Map p90, C3

If you're a Korean-food virgin, this hip hang-out is a fine place to lose your innocence. There are classics like *bibimbap* (a hot-pot rice dish), but most people opt for the barbecue, grilled at table and paired with tasty *panchan* (side dishes). Elevated tolerance for spiciness required. (📞0163 458 0203; www.kimchiprincess.com; Skalitzer Strasse 36; mains €8.50-23.50; ⏱dinner; U-Bahn Görlitzer Bahnhof)

Burgermeister
AMERICAN €

8 Map p90, G2

It's green, ornate, a century old and... it used to be a toilet. Now it's a burger joint below the elevated U-Bahn tracks serving plump all-beef patties and great fries with classic, home-made dips (peanut, mango-curry). (Oberbaumstrasse 8; burgers €3-4; ⏱11am-2am or later; U-Bahn Schlesisches Tor)

Il Casolare
PIZZERIA €

9 Map p90, A4

The pizzas here are truly dynamite – thin, crispy, cheap and wagon-wheel-sized – and the canalside beer garden an idyllic spot to gobble 'em up. (Grimmstrasse 30; pizzas €6-9; ⏱noon-midnight; U-Bahn Schönleinstrasse)

Drinking

Club der Visionäre
BAR, CLUB

10 Map p90, H4

It's drinks, pizza and fine electro at this summertime chill and party play-ground in an old canalside boatshed. Hang out beneath the weeping willows or stake out some turf on the upstairs deck. On weekends party people invade 24/7. Toilets suck. (www.clubder visionaere.com, in German; Am Flutgraben 1; ⏱from 2pm Mon-Fri, from noon Sat & Sun, usually May-Sep; U-Bahn Schlesisches Tor)

Watergate
CLUB

11 Map p90, G2

It's a short night's journey into day at this high-octane riverside club with

---

✅ Top Tip

Party Strips

Aside from Kottbusser Tor, Oranienstrasse and Schlesische Strasse are both established tipple drags but Wiener Strasse and especially Skalitzer Strasse are catching up.

Understand

Techno Town Berlin

Techno may have its roots in Detroit-based house music, but it was from Berlin that it conquered the world. Dr Motte and DJ Westbam, who both had commercial success with house and electro sounds, are considered two of the 'godfathers' of the Berlin techno sound. In 1987–88, they played their first DJ gigs at the UFO – the city's first (and illegal) techno club – and cofounded the now defunct Love Parade.

When the second UFO club closed in 1991, the techno-sonic brotherhood moved on to mega-venues E-Werk and Tresor, which launched camouflage-wearing Berlin superstar DJ Tanith along with trance pioneer Paul van Dyk. The Tresor label has since become an international brand with a full range of merchandising. Other early artists include Marusha, whose 1994 mega-hit *Somewhere over the Rainbow* ushered in the commercialisation of dance music. Other DJs kept it more real, most famously BPitch label cofounder Ellen Allien.

These days, pure techno has essentially been sidelined as more and more splinter genres of electronic music percolate in the club scene. House is not as ubiquitous in Berlin as it is in the rest of Europe and the USA, but it does dominate uber-hip spaces like the Panorama Bar (p108) and Cookies (p37).

Another offshoot is breakbeat, which has travelled east from the UK. The local label currently leading the pack is Shitkatapult, whose main artist Apparat's experiments with sound and vocals result in vivid, melodic techno and rich electropop. Apparat has also been involved in various collaborations, for instance with the duo Modeselektor. Another internationally known DJ is Paul Kalkbrenner who, in 2008, starred in the semi-autobiographical flick *Berlin Calling*.

There's also the heavyweight label collective Get Physical, whose artist roster includes the dynamic DJ duo M.A.N.D.Y., known for infusing house and electro with minimal and funk.

An excellent movie about Germany's early techno scene and culture is *We Call it Techno!*, released by Sense Music & Media (www.sense music.de).

two floors, panoramic windows and a floating terrace overlooking the Oberbaumbrücke and Universal Music. A killer electro line-up keeps the clued-in hot and sweaty. Long queues, tight door on weekends. (www.water-gate.de; Falckensteinstrasse 49a; ⏱Thu-Sat; U-Bahn Schlesisches Tor)

Madame Claude
BAR, LIVE MUSIC

12 ⓦ Map p90, F3

Gravity is literally upended at this David Lynch-ian booze burrow where the furniture dangles from the ceiling and the moulding's on the floor. Don't worry, there are still comfy sofas for slouching and entertaining your posse, plus Wednesday's music quiz, live music or DJs and open-mike Sundays. (Lübbener Strasse 19; U-Bahn Schlesisches Tor, Görlitzer Bahnhof)

Freischwimmer
CAFE, BAR

13 ⓦ Map p90, H3

Few places are more idyllic than this rustic 1930s boathouse turned all-day canalside chill zone. Come for chit-chat, a cold beer, a pick from the global menu or Sunday brunch. (www .freischwimmer-berlin.de, in German; Vor dem Schlesischen Tor 2a; ⏱from 4pm Mon-Fri, from 10am Sat & Sun, check for winter hours; U-Bahn Schlesisches Tor)

Ankerklause
PUB

14 ⓦ Map p90, B4

Ahoy there! This nautical kitsch tavern with an ass-kicking jukebox sets sail in an old harbour-master's shack and is great for quaffing and waving to the boats puttering along the canal. Breakfast and snacks provide sustenance. (www.ankerklause.de, in German; Kottbusser Damm 104; ⏱from 4pm Mon, from 9am Tue-Sun; U-Bahn Schönleinstrasse)

Entertainment

Magnet
LIVE MUSIC, CLUB

15 ⭐ Map p90, G2

This indie and alt-sound bastion is known for bookers with an astronomer's ability to detect stars in the making. After the last riff, the mostly student-age crowd hits the dance floor to – depending on the night – Britpop, indietronics, neodisco, rock and punk. (www.magnet-club.de, in German; Falckensteinstrasse 48; ⏱Tue-Sat; U-Bahn Schlesisches Tor)

Lido
LIVE MUSIC, CLUB

16 ⭐ Map p90, G3

A 1950s cinema has been recycled into a rock-indie-electro-pop mecca with mosh-pit electricity and a crowd that cares more about the music than about looking good. Global DJs and talented upwardly mobile live noise-makers pull in the punters. Legendary Balkanbeats parties, too. (www.lido -berlin.de, in German; Cuvrystrasse 7; U-Bahn Schlesisches Tor)

Q Local Life
All Aboard the Badeschiff

Take an old river barge, fill with water, moor in the Spree River and voila: the **Badeschiff** (Map p90, H3; www.arena-berlin.de, in German; Eichenstrasse 4), the preferred swim-and-tan spot for Berlin kool kids. After-dark action includes parties, bands, movies and simply hanging out. In winter it's all covered up and turned into a deliciously toasty chill zone with saunas and lounge bar.

Shopping

Killerbeast
FASHION

17 🔒 Map p90, G3

'Kill uniformity' is the motto of this boutique where Claudia and her colleagues make new clothes from old ones right in the back of the store. No two pieces are alike, prices are very reasonable and there's even a line for kids. (www.killerbeast.de, in German; Schlesische Strasse 31; ⏱3-8pm Mon, 1-8pm Tue-Fri, 1-5pm Sat; U-Bahn Schlesisches Tor)

Overkill
FASHION

18 🔒 Map p90, F2

What started as a graffiti magazine back in 1992 has evolved into one of Germany's top spots for sneakers and streetwear. Browse an entire wall of limited-editions by such cult purveyors as Onitsuka Tiger, Converse and Asics (including vegan versions) alongside import threads by Stüssy, KidRobot, Darkhorse, Cake and MHI. (www.overkill.de; Köpenicker Strasse 195a; U-Bahn Schlesisches Tor)

UKO Fashion
FASHION

19 🔒 Map p90, C3

High quality at low prices is the magic formula that has garnered this uncluttered clothing store a loyal clientele. It's a veritable gold mine for the latest girl threads by Pussy Deluxe and Muchacha, secondhand items from Esprit to Zappa, and hot-label samples by Vero Moda, only and boyco. (www.uko-fashion.de, in German; Oranienstrasse 201; ⏱11am-8pm Mon-Fri, to 4pm Sat; U-Bahn Görlitzer Bahnhof)

Hardwax
MUSIC

20 🔒 Map p90, B3

This well-hidden outpost has been on the cutting edge of electronic music for about two decades and is a must-stop for fans of techno, house, minimal and dubstep. (www.hardwax.com; 3rd fl, door A, 2nd courtyard, Paul-Lincke-Ufer 44a; ⏱noon-8pm Mon-Sat; U-Bahn Kottbusser Tor)

Local Life
Nosing Around Neukölln

Getting There

Kreuzkölln is just south of Kreuzberg, separated from it by the Landwehrkanal.

U-Bahn Start at Schönleinstrasse (U8). The closest stop to the finish line is Karl-Marx-Strasse (U7).

Northern Neukölln is booming. Once making headlines for its high crime rate and poor schools, this multicultural district just south of Kreuzberg is now Berlin's latest frontier of hipness. Also known as Kreuzkölln, it has seen an explosion of trash-trendy cafes, bars and art and performance spaces with a thriving DIY ethos. Come now for a delightful off-the-beaten-track experience. Turbo-gentrification may be waiting in the wings.

❶ Cafe Jacques

A favourite with off-duty chefs and local foodies, **Cafe Jacques** (☎694 1048; Maybachufer 8; mains €10-16; ☻dinner) infallibly charms with flattering candlelight, warm decor, fantastic wine and a French and North African–inspired menu. Reservations de rigeur.

❷ Türkenmarkt

Berlin goes Bosporus at this lively canalside **farmers market** (Maybachufer; ☻noon-6.30pm Tue & Fri) perfect for putting together yummy picnics from buckets of olives, creamy cheese spreads, crusty flatbread and some of the freshest bargain-priced produce around. Grab your loot and head west to find a nice place along the canal.

❸ Hüttenpalast

An old vacuum-cleaner factory, **Hüttenpalast** (www.huettenpalast.de; Hobrechtstrasse 66; ☻8am-6pm Mon-Sat, to 4pm Sun) is a hotel and playground where you can sleep in old campervans or wooden huts. Kick back in the garden among an exuberant idyll of herbs, vines and vegetables or enjoy an organic breakfast, meat-free lunch and homemade cakes in the cafe.

❹ Sauvage

Sign up for a wild time at Berlin's first Paleo restaurant, stylishly set up in a former brothel. Yup, at **Sauvage** (www .sauvageberlin.com; Pflügerstrasse 25; mains €10-20; ☻dinner Tue-Sun) you'll be eating like it was 10,000 BC: no grains, cheese or sugar but all-organic dishes featuring fish, meat, eggs, herbs, seeds, oils, fruit and wild vegetables.

❺ Berlin Burger International

Size matters at **BBI** (www.berlinburger international.com; Pannierstrasse 5; burgers from €3.90; ☻1-11pm). At least when it comes to their burgers: handmade, two-fisted, bulging, sloppy contenders.

❻ Ä

A dinosaur by Neukölln pub standards, **Ä** (www.ae-neukoelln.de, in German; Weserstrasse 40; ☻from 5pm) is still a fine, dressed-down place to feed your party animal. Expect to be eclectically entertained by pinball machines, DJs, live bands or a monthly live soap opera starring cast-off stuffed toys.

❼ Sameheads

An ingenious shop-cafe-bar-club-party-space, **Sameheads** (www.same heads.com; Richardstrasse 10; ☻11am-late) stocks boho fashions by emerging designers but extends its subculture synergy to weird-cinema nights, a hilarious pub quiz, all-you-can-eat buffet dinners and funky parties.

❽ Neuköllner Oper

Definitely not your upper-crust opera house, the **Neuköllner Oper** (☎688 9070; www.neukoellneroper.de, in German; Karl-Marx-Strasse 131-133), in a refurbished pre-war ballroom, has an actively anti-elitist repertoire ranging from intelligent musical theatre to original productions to experimental interpretations of classic works.

Explore

Friedrichshain

Rents may be rising and gentrification unstoppable, but for now there's still plenty of partying to be done in this student-heavy district. Soak up the socialist vibe on Karl-Marx-Allee and revel in post-reunification euphoria at the East Side Gallery before finding your favourite libation station(s) around Boxhagener Platz. Wrap up the night with a dedicated dance-a-thon in a top techno club.

The Sights in a Day

☀ Make your way to Ostbahnhof and confront the ghosts of the Cold War on a stroll along the **East Side Gallery** (pictured left; p102). After giving your camera a workout, either pop into the cafe at **Universal Music** (p103) for a late-morning pick-me-up or report straight to **Michelberger** (p106) for lunch.

☀ Following lunch, walk over to **Karl-Marx-Allee** (p106). You'll feel like Gulliver in the land of Brobdingnag when parading along this phalanx of monumental buildings, some clad in Meissen tiles. Drop by **Café Sybille** (p106) to learn more about this GDR-era showcase boulevard before hopping on the U5 at Strausberger Platz. Ride the three stops to Samariterstrasse and head towards Boxhagener Platz for an aimless wander, poking into boho boutiques, grabbing ice cream from **Caramello** (p108) or watching kids at play.

☾ Reflect upon the day's events over locally brewed Pilsner at **Hops & Barley** (p107), then waltz over to **Schwarzer Hahn** (p106) for upmarket German home-cooking in low-key surroundings. Wrap up the evening with a fat glass of Bordeaux at **Place Clichy** (p107) or cocktails at **Süss war Gestern** (p108).

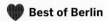

◉ Top Sights

East Side Gallery (p102)

🖤 Best of Berlin

Eating
Schwarzer Hahn (p106)

Bars
Strandgut Berlin (p108)
Süss War Gestern (p108)

Clubs
Berghain/Panorama Bar (p108)
://about blank (p108)

Live Music
Astra Kulturhaus (p109)

Gay & Lesbian
Zum Schmutzigen Hobby (p108)
Himmelreich (p109)
Berghain (p108)

Getting There

S-Bahn Warschauer Strasse (S3, S5, S7/75, S9) is the most central stop.

🚋 **Tram** The M13 goes from Warschauer Strasse station to Boxhagener Platz.

U-Bahn Frankfurter Tor (U5) and Warschauer Strasse (U1) are your best bets.

Top Sights
East Side Gallery

The year was 1989. After 28 years, the Berlin
Wall, that grim divider of humanity, finally met
its maker. Most of it was quickly dismantled, but
along Mühlenstrasse, paralleling the Spree River,
a 1.3km stretch became the East Side Gallery,
the world's largest open-air mural collection. In
more than 100 paintings, dozens of international
artists translated the era's global euphoria and
optimism into a mix of political statements, drug-
induced musings and truly artistic visions. It was
restored in 2009.

👁 Map p104, C4

www.eastsidegallery
-berlin.de

Mühlenstrasse btwn
Oberbaumbrücke &
Ostbahnhof

admission free

⏱24hr

U-/S-Bahn Warschauer
Strasse; S-Bahn
Ostbahnhof

Don't Miss

Dimitry Vrubel: My God, help me survive amid this deadly love

The gallery's best-known painting, showing Soviet and GDR leaders Leonid Brezhnev and Erich Honecker locking lips with eyes closed, is based on an actual photograph taken by French journalist Regis Bossu during Brezhnev's 1979 Berlin visit. This kind of kiss was an expression of great respect in socialist countries.

Birgit Kinder: Test the Rest

Another shutterbug favourite is Birgit Kinder's painting of a GDR-era Trabant car (known as a Trabi) bursting through the Wall with the licence plate reading 'NOV•9–89', the day the barrier was shattered.

Kani Alavi: It Happened in November

A wave of people being squeezed through a breached Wall in a metaphorical rebirth reflects Kani Alavi's recollection of the events of 9 November. Note the facial expressions, ranging from hope, joy and euphoria to disbelief and fear.

Thierry Noir: Homage to the Young Generation

French artist Thierry Noir's boldly coloured cartoon-like heads symbolise the new-found freedom after the Wall's collapse.

Thomas Klingenstein: Detour to the Japanese Sector

Born in East Berlin, Thomas Klingenstein spent time in a Stasi prison for dissent before being extradited to West Germany in 1980. This mural was inspired by his childhood love for Japan, where he ended up living from 1984 to the mid-'90s.

☑ Top Tips

▶ The more-famous paintings are near the Ostbahnhof end, so start your walk here if you've only got limited time.

▶ For more street art, check out the river-facing side of the Wall.

▶ Meet friendly locals and expats at the World Language Party held every Wednesday from 7pm on the Eastern Comfort Hostel Boat, moored neared Ober-baumbrücke.

✕ Take a Break

Wiggle your toes in the sand of Strandgut Berlin (p108), just one of several riverside beach bars behind the East Side Gallery.

Mingle with media types for coffee, snacks or a hot lunch in the river-side cafe of **Universal Music** (Map p104, D5; Stralauer Allee 1; ⏱8am-8pm Mon-Fri Apr-Sep, to 6pm Oct-Mar).

A

B

C

D

1 Ⓤ Strausberger Platz

Weidenweg

Weberwiese Ⓤ

Karl-Marx-A

Krautstr

Singerstr

Rüdersdorfer

Strasse der Pariser Kommune

Franz-Mehring-Platz

Marchlewskistr

Gubener Str

2

Andreasstr

Koppenstr

Wriezener Karree

Wedekindstr

Rüdersdorfer Str

Corneliusplat

Ⓡ Ostbahnhof

Ⓢ 12

Ⓢ Ostbahnhof

Strasse der Pariser Kommune

An der Ostbahn

Helsingforser Str

3

Am Ostbahnhof

Stralauer Platz

Schillingbrücke

FRIEDRICHSHAIN

Helsingfor Pl.

Mühlenstr

Helen-Ernst-Str

4

11 Ⓢ

Mildred-Harnack-Str

O2 World

Hedwig-Wachenheim-Str

Tamara-Danz-Str

East Side Gallery
◉

16
Ⓢ
Warschauer Ⓤ
Str Ⓢ

Manteuffelstr

0 ——— 400 m
0 ——— 0.2 miles

Ⓝ

4 Ⓢ

Warschauer Pla

Spree River

Köpenicker Str

Am Oberbaum

Stralauer

5

For reviews see	
◉ Top Sights	p102
◎ Sights	p106
⊗ Eating	p106
⬤ Drinking	p107
★ Entertainment	p109
⬢ Shopping	p109

Schlesisches Tor Ⓤ

Oberbaumbrücke

E

F

G

H

1

Bänschstr

Rigaer Str

Proskauer Str

🔒19

Schreinerstr

Samariterstr

Frankfurter Tor

1 Ⓤ

arl-Marx- Allee

Frankfurter Allee

Ⓤ Samariterstr

Niederbarnimstr

Mainzer Str

2

Boxhagener Str

rünberger Str

Weichselstr

Simon-Dach-Str

Gabriel-Max-Str

Gärtnerstr

5 ✗

🔒 18

Kopernikusstr

15 🔒

Boxhagener Platz

Krossener Str

Holteistr

6 ✗

3

Wühlischstr

Simon-Dach-Str

2 ✗

3 ✗ 7 🔒

Simplonstr

Seumestr

9 🔒 8 🔒

10 🔒

chauer Str

✗17

Revaler Str

Sonntagstr

14 🔒

4

Lenbachstr

Neue Bahnhofstr

Rudolfstr

Modersohnstr

Rotherstr

Rudolfplatz

Ⓢ Ostkreuz

5

Corinthstr

13 🔒

Hauptstr

Top Tip

Spotlight on KMA

For more background on the Karl-Marx-Allee (KMA), drop by **Café Sybille** (Map p104, B1; Karl-Marx-Allee 72; admission free; 10am-8pm Mon-Fri, noon-8pm Sat & Sun), which has coffee as well as an excellent exhibit charting the milestones of the boulevard from inception to today.

Sights

Karl-Marx-Allee   HISTORIC SITE

1 ◎ Map p104, E1

This monumental boulevard is one of Berlin's most impressive GDR-era relics. At 90m wide, the Karl-Marx-Allee (KMA) was built between 1952 and 1960 and runs for 2.3km between Alexanderplatz and Frankfurter Tor. A source of considerable East German pride, it provided modern flats and served as a backdrop for vast military parades. (U-Bahn Strausberger Platz, Weberwiese, Frankfurter Tor)

Eating

Schwarzer Hahn   GERMAN €€

2 ✕ Map p104, G3

This personable slow-food bistro shines the spotlight on regionally sourced German soul food, elegantly updated for the 21st century. Service is impeccable and the staff know a thing or two about wine. (✆2197 0371; Seumestrasse 23; mains €8-20; lunch Mon-Fri, dinner Mon-Sat; U-/S-Bahn Warschauer Strasse; U-Bahn Samariterstrasse; S-Bahn Ostkreuz; ☒M13)

Spätzle & Knödel   GERMAN €€

3 ✕ Map p104, G3

Get your southern German comfort-food fix at this elbows-on-the-table gastropub. The decor ain't much but all is forgiven when tucking into waist-expanding portions of roast pork, goulash and the eponymous *Kässpätzle* (German mac 'n' cheese) and *knödel* (dumplings). Bonus: Augustiner, Riegele and Unertl on tap. (✆2757 1151; Wühlischstrasse 20; mains €8-15; dinner; U-/S-Bahn Warschauer Strasse; U-Bahn Samariterstrasse; S-Bahn Ostkreuz; ☒M13)

Michelberger   MEDITERRANEAN €

4 ✕ Map p104, D5

One of Berlin's hippest hotels, Michelberger does weekday lunches to feed hungry desk jockeys and East Side Gallery visitors in an airy, tiled dining room. Dishes change daily but always have a Mediterranean streak as exemplified by ratatouille, polenta and creative pastas. (Warschauer Strasse 39-40; mains €5-10; noon-2.30pm Mon-Fri; U-/S-Bahn Warschauer Strasse; �)

Lemon Leaf   VIETNAMESE €

5 ✕ Map p104, F3

Cheap and cheerful, this place is always swarmed by loyal local hipsters and for good reason: light, inventive and fresh, the Indo-Chinese menu

has few false notes. The modest list of options is supplemented by daily specials, and the homemade mango lassi is rave-worthy. (Grünberger Strasse 69; mains €5-9; U-Bahn Frankfurter Tor)

Burgeramt   AMERICAN €

6 ⊗ Map p104, F3

You may need to pack a little patience at this beloved patty provider but the juiciness is worth the wait. (Krossener Strasse 22; mains €3-5; ⊗noon-1am; U-Bahn Frankfurter Tor; U-/S-Bahn Warschauer Strasse)

Drinking

Hops & Barley   PUB

7 ⊙ Map p104, G3

Conversation flows as freely as the unfiltered Pilsner, malty dark, fruity wheat beer and potent cider produced right at this congenial microbrewery inside a former butcher shop. Share a table with low-key locals swilling after-work pints among ceramic-tiled walls and shiny copper vats. (www .hopsandbarley-berlin.de, in German; Wühlischstrasse 22-23; U-/S-Bahn Warschauer Strasse; U-Bahn Samariterstrasse; S-Bahn Ostkreuz; 🚋M13)

Kptn A Müller   PUB

8 ⊙ Map p104, F3

Arrgh matey, the captain's in town, bringing much-needed relief from the cookie-cutter cocktail-lounge circuit. Pretentions are checked at the door of this self-service joint where drinks are cheap and foosball and wi-fi free. (www .kptn.de, in German; Simon-Dach-Strasse 32; U-/S-Bahn Warschauer Strasse; 🛜)

Place Clichy   BAR

9 ⊙ Map p104, E3

Chapeau! Clichy brings a whiff of Paris to the lower end of Simon-Dach-Strasse. Candlelit, artist-designed and cosy, the postage-stamp-sized wine bar exudes an almost existentialist vibe, so don your black turtleneck and join the chatty crowd for Bordeaux and sweaty cheeses. (Simon-Dach-Strasse 22; ⊙Tue-Sat; U-/S-Bahn Warschauer Strasse; 🚋M10, M13)

Oberbaumbrücke bridge over the Spree River

Local Life
Dreamy Ice Cream

There's ice cream and then there's **Caramello** (Map p104, F3; Wühlischstrasse 31; ⏱from 11am; U-/S-Bahn Warschauer Strasse). Join the inevitable queue for over 40 varieties of tastebud-teasers ranging from pistachio to bitter orange, all of them organic and homemade. There are soy-based concoctions for vegans and the lactose-intolerant, plus strong coffees and tempting sweets.

Süss War Gestern   BAR

10 🚇 Map p104, G4

Chilled electro and well-mixed cocktails put you in a mellow mood and the low light makes everyone look good. Only problem: once you're swallowed by the plush retro sofa it may be hard to get up to order that next drink. Try the eponymous house cocktail made with real root ginger, ginger ale and whisky. Smoking OK. (Wühlischstrasse 43; ⏱from 8pm Mon-Sat; U-/S-Bahn Warschauer Strasse; U-Bahn Samariterstrasse; 🚌M10, M13)

Strandgut Berlin   BEACH BAR

11 🚇 Map p104, B4

Drink a toast to Berlin at the chicest of the East Side Gallery sandpits where the beer is cold, the cocktails strong, the crowd grown-up and the DJs tops. (www.strandgut-berlin.com, in German; Mühlenstrasse 61-63; ⏱from 10am; S-Bahn Ostbahnhof; 🛜)

Berghain/Panorama Bar   CLUB

12 🚇 Map p104, C3

Only world-class spinmasters heat up this hedonistic bass-junkie hellhole inside a labyrinthine ex-power plant. Upstairs, Panorama Bar pulsates with house and electro, while the big factory floor below (Berghain) is gay-leaning and hard techno. Strict door and no cameras. (www.berghain.de; Am Wriezener Bahnhof; ⏱Fri & Sat; S-Bahn Ostbahnhof)

://about blank   CLUB

13 🚇 Map p104, G5

This club collective also organises cultural and political events that often segue into long, intense club nights when talented DJs feed a diverse bunch of revellers with danceworthy electronic gruel. If you get the spirit of openness and tolerance, you'll have a grand old time here. (www.aboutparty.net, in German; Markgrafendamm 24c; ⏱Thu-Sat; S-Bahn Ostkreuz)

Zum Schmutzigen Hobby   GAY BAR

14 🚇 Map p104, F4

Berlin's trash-drag deity Nina Queer has flown her long-time Prenzlauer Berg coop and reopened her louche den of kitsch and glam in less hostile environs amid the Friedrichshain kool kids. Wednesday's 'Glamour Trivia Quiz' is legendary. (www.ninaqueer.com; Revaler Strasse 99, RAW, gate 2; U-/S-Bahn Warschauer Strasse)

Himmelreich

GAY BAR

15 Map p104, F3

Confirming all those stereotypes about gays having good taste, this smart red-hued cocktail bar cum retro-style lounge makes most of the competition look like a straight guy's bedsit. Tuesdays are women-only and on Wednesdays drinks are 2-4-1. (www.himmelreich -berlin.de, in German; Simon-Dach-Strasse 36; U-/S-Bahn Warschauer Strasse)

Monster Ronson's Ichiban Karaoke

KARAOKE

16 Map p104, D4

Knock back a couple of brewskis if you need to loosen your nerves before belting out your best Abba or Lady Gaga at this mad, great karaoke joint. *Pop Idol* wannabes can hit the stage; shy types may prefer music and mischief in a private party room. (☎8975 1327; www.karaokemonster.de, in German; Warschauer Strasse 34; U-/S-Bahn Warschauer Strasse)

Entertainment

Astra Kulturhaus

LIVE MUSIC

17 Map p104, E4

With space for 1500, Astra is one of the biggest indie spaces in town, yet often fills up easily, and not just for such headliners as Melissa Etheridge, Kasabian and the Eels. Bonus: the supersweet '50s GDR decor. Beer garden in summer. (www.astra-berlin.de, in German; Revaler Strasse 99; U-/S-Bahn Warschauer Strasse)

Shopping

Flohmarkt am Boxhagener Platz

FLEA MARKET

18 Map p104, F3

Wrapped around leafy Boxhagener Platz, this fun flea market is just a java-whiff away from Sunday brunch cafes. Among vendors it's easy to sniff out the pros from the regular folk here to unload their spring-cleaning detritus for pennies. (Boxhagener Platz; ⏱10am-6pm Sun; U-/S-Bahn Warschauer Strasse; U-Bahn Frankfurter Tor)

Mondos Arts

GIFTS, SOUVENIRS

19 Map p104, G1

Cult and kitsch seem to be the GDR's strongest survivors at this funky little shop, named after Mondos, a brand of condoms. It's fun to have a look even if you didn't grow up drinking Red October beer, falling asleep to the *Sandmännchen* (Little Sandman) TV show or listening to rock by the Puhdys. (www.mondosarts.de, in German; Schreinerstrasse 6; ⏱noon-7pm Mon-Fri, 6pm Sat; U-Bahn Samariterstrasse)

Explore

Prenzlauer Berg

Prenzlauer Berg went from rags to riches after reunification and emerged as one of Berlin's most desirable residential neighbourhoods. Its ample charms are best experienced on a leisurely meander. Look up at gorgeously restored townhouses, comb side streets for indie boutiques or carve out a spot in a charismatic cafe. On Sundays, the Mauerpark is a heaving haven of fun and flea-market browsing.

The Sights in a Day

A perfect start to the day is the irresistible combo of strong coffee and delicious breakfast at **Anna Blume** (p119), preferably seated at a sidewalk table. Spend the rest of the morning strolling down to Kollwitz-platz and its side streets, popping into boutiques stocked with classy fashions, designer furnishings, organic baby clothing, handmade chocolates and whatever else the local hearts desire. Walk north via leafy Husemannstrasse and admire the red-brick architecture of the **Kulturbrauerei** (p120).

Order a Currywurst (curried sausage) at **Konnopke's Imbiss** (p118) and decide for yourself whether the long queues are justified. Put in a bit more shopping along Kastanienallee and Oderberger Strasse, then head over to the **Mauerpark** (p112) and try to visualise what it looked like when the Berlin Wall ran through it.

Make your way back to Kastanienallee and stake out a beer table beneath the towering chestnuts of **Prater** (p118), Berlin's oldest beer garden. For dinner, either walk around the corner to **Oderquelle** (p117) or – for an even more local experience – hoof it over to **Frau Mittenmang** (p116).

For a local's day in Prenzlauer Berg, see p112.

Local Life

Sundays Around the Mauerpark (p112)

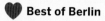 Best of Berlin

Eating
Frau Mittenmang (p116)

W – der Imbiss (p118)

Schusterjunge (p118)

Oderquelle (p117)

Shopping
Mauerpark Flea Market (p113)

Flohmarkt am Arkonaplatz (p120)

Ta(u)sche (p121)

Erfinderladen Berlin (p120)

Luxus International (p121)

Getting There

S-Bahn The main hub is Schönhauser Allee station (S8, S9, S41 and S42).

Tram The most useful line is the M1, which links to Mitte via Schönhauser Allee and Kastanienallee.

U-Bahn The U2 comes up from Alexanderplatz. The best jumping-off point for the area is Eberswalder Strasse station.

Local Life
Sundays Around the Mauerpark

Long-time locals, neo-Berliners and the international tourist brigade – everyone flocks to the Mauerpark on Sundays. It's a wild and wacky urban tapestry where a flea market, outdoor karaoke, artists and bands provide entertainment and people gather for barbecue, basketball, badminton and boules. A graffiti-covered section of the Berlin Wall, which once bisected the park, quietly looms above it all.

❶ **Bright Beginnings**

Start your day on Oderberger Strasse, with breakfast at **Hüftengold** (Oderberger Strasse 27) or waffles at **Kauf Dich Glücklich** (Oderberger Strasse 44). The street's beautifully restored 19th-century townhouses were saved from demolition by locals in the late '70s. Recently, neighbours again banded together to prevent old trees from falling victim to another street revamp.

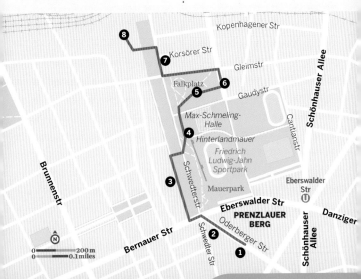

❷ Coffee Deluxe

If Synesso Cyncra and 'third wave coffee' are not mere gobbledygook to you, you speak the language of Kiduk and Yumi, owners of the pocket-size shrine for javaholics called **Bonanza Coffee Heroes** (Oderberger Strasse 35; ⏱8.30am-7pm Mon-Fri, from 10am Sat & Sun). All beans are roasted on-site in an antique roasting machine.

❸ Urban Archaeology

Fed and caffeinated, you're now ready to join the throngs of thrifty trinket hunters, bleary-eyed clubbers and excited visitors sifting for treasure at the vibrant **Mauerpark Flea Market** (⏱10am-7pm Sun). Source new favourites among the retro threads, local-designer T-shirts, communist memorabilia, vintage vinyl and offbeat stuff. Ethnic food stands and beer gardens provide sustenance.

❹ Bearpit Karaoke

Berlin's greatest free entertainment kicks off at 3pm when Joe Hatchiban sets up his custom-made mobile karaoke unit in the Mauerpark's amphitheatre. As many as 2000 people cram onto the stone bleachers to cheer and clap for eager crooners ranging from giggling 11-year-olds to Broadway-calibre belters. Give generously when Joe passes the coffee can, for this show must go on forever. Summer only.

❺ Falkplatz

Flashback to 1825 and picture Prussian soldiers parading around what is now a leafy park studded with ancient chestnut, oak, birch, ash and poplar trees. Relax on the grass and watch kids frolicking around the sea-lion fountain, then search for other animal sculptures tucked among the shrubs.

❻ Burgermania

New York meets Berlin at the **Bird** (www.thebirdinberlin.com; Am Falkplatz 5; mains €9.50-13; ⏱6pm-midnight Mon-Fri, from noon Sat & Sun), a buzzy gastropub known for its killer burgers. Sink your teeth into a dripping half-pounder made from freshly ground steak between a toasted English muffin.

❼ Neighbourhood Cafe

On a sunny day, the terrace of **Cafe Niesen** (Korsörer Strasse 13; dishes €1.50-7; ⏱10am-10pm Apr-Oct, to 8pm Nov-Mar) is a popular stop for coffee, homemade cakes, breakfast and snacks or a glass of 'Niesonade', a refreshing blend of elderberries, lemon and mineral water. Families love it here, but there's also an adult-only room for sipping lattes in quiet.

❽ Northern Mauerpark

To escape the Mauerpark frenzy and see where the locals relax, head to the park's extension north of Gleimstrasse. This is also where you'll find the Jugendhof Moritzdorf, an educational farm playground complete with barnyard animals. Further along you can watch daredevils scale the 'Schwedter Northface', a climbing wall operated by the German Alpine Club.

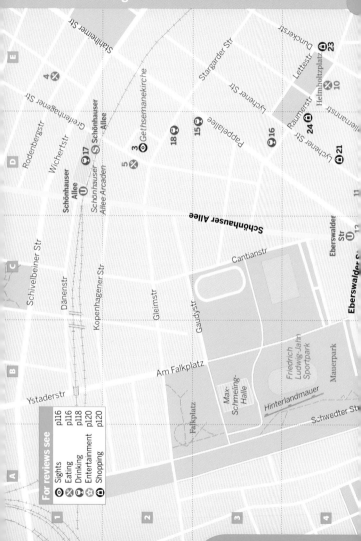

Prenzlauer Allee

Christburger Str

Rykestr

Marienburger Str

Danziger Str

Husemannstr

9 ⊗

Sredzkistr

14 ⊙

Kollwitzplatz

1 ⊙

Knaackstr

Kollwitzstr

Wörther Str

2 ⊙ Jüdischer Friedhof
Schönhauser Allee

Belforter Str

Strassburger Str

Metzer Str

N ⊙

Saarbrücker Str

Schönhauser Allee

Schwedter Str

Senefelderplatz Ⓤ

19 Ⓤ

20 ✿

26 ⊕

13 ⊙ PRENZLAUER
BERG

6 ⊗

Oderberger Str

Teutoburger
Platz

25 ⊙

Choriner Str

27 ⊡

Kastanienallee

Schwedter Str

8 ⊗

Weinbergsweg

Arkonaplatz

22 ⊡

Ruppinerstr

Zionskirchplatz

Fehrbelliner Str

Veteranenstr

Volkspark am
Weinbergsweg

Bernauer Str

Brunnenstr

Rosenthaler
Platz Ⓤ

7 ⊗

400 m
0.2 miles

0   0

Sights

Kollwitzplatz
SQUARE

1 ⊙ Map p114, D6

This parklike triangular square was ground zero of Prenzlauer Berg's revitalisation. Grab a cafe table and watch the leagues of yoga mamas, greying hipsters and gawking tourists on parade. Kids burn energy on the playgrounds or while clambering over a bronze sculpture of the square's namesake, artist Käthe Kollwitz (p126). A great time to visit is during the Thursday or Saturday farmers markets. (U-Bahn Senefelderplatz)

Jüdischer Friedhof Schönhauser Allee
CEMETERY

2 ⊙ Map p114, D7

Berlin's second Jewish cemetery opened in 1827 and hosts such famous dearly departed as the artist Max Liebermann and the composer Giacomo Meyerbeer. WWII brought vandalism but it's still a pretty place with dappled light filtering through big old trees. (Schönhauser Allee 22; ⊙8am-4pm Mon-Thu, 7.30am-2.30pm Fri; U-Bahn Senefelderplatz)

Gethsemanekirche
CHURCH

3 ⊙ Map p114, D2

This 1893 neo-Gothic church was a hotbed of dissent in the final days of the GDR and thus a thorn in the side of the Stasi which, as late as October 1989, brutally quashed a peaceful gathering outside the church.

Ernst Barlach's *Geistkämpfer* (Ghost Fighter; 1928) sculpture stands on the church's south side. (www .gethsemanekirche.de; Stargarder Strasse 77; U-/S-Bahn Schönhauser Allee)

Eating

Frau Mittenmang
MODERN GERMAN €€

4 ✕ Map p114, E1

This unhurried neighbourhood-adored restaurant with sidewalk seating delivers a daily changing menu that folds international influences into classic German dishes. Hunker down at a polished wooden table and join locals for meals, the house brew or a glass of excellent wine. (✆444 5654; www.fraumittenmang.de, in German; Rodenbergstrasse 37; mains €9-17; ⊙dinner; U-/S-Bahn Schönhauser Allee; ◻M1, 12)

Q Local Life
Knaackstrasse Cafe Scene

Mere steps from Kollwitzplatz, pretty Knaackstrasse is a quiet residential street with a row of charming cafes and restaurants, including **Pasternak** (Map p114, E7; www.restaurant-pasternak.de; Knaack-strasse 22-24; mains €11-21; ⊙9am-1am) for Russian and **La Poulette** (Map p114, D7; www.poulette.de; Knaackstrasse 30-32; mains €16-25) for French. It's a great spot for sipping your latte at a sunny sidewalk table and watching the world on parade.

Prater (p118)

A Magica PIZZERIA €€

5 Map p114, D2

This always-packed joint consistently delivers Neapolitan pizzas with pizazz straight out of the wood-burning oven. They go down well with luscious red house wine served in water glasses. Come early before local groupies have snapped up all the tables. (Greifenhagener Strasse 54; pizzas €5-10; ⏰4pm-midnight; U-Bahn Schönhauser Allee; 🚋M1)

Oderquelle GERMAN €€

6 Map p114, B5

It's always fun to pop by this woodsy resto and see what's inspired the chef today. Most likely, it'll be a delicious well-crafted German meal, perhaps with a slight Mediterranean nuance.

The generously topped and crispy *Flammekuche* (French pizzas) are a reliable standby. Excellent wines, too. (📞4400 8080; Oderberger Strasse 27; mains €10-19; ⏰dinner daily, lunch Sun; U-Bahn Eberswalder Strasse)

Zagreus Projekt INTERNATIONAL €€€

7 Map p114, A8

Art meets food in this project space headed by chef-artist-gallery-owner Ulrich Krauss. Every other month, Krauss invites a different artist to create a site-specific installation, then composes a menu around it and serves it at a long communal table. Great for art-loving foodies and food-loving artists. Reservations required. (📞2809 5640; www.zagreus.net; Brunnenstrasse 9a; 4-course dinner €35; U-Bahn Rosenthaler Platz)

W – der Imbiss

FUSION €

8 | Map p114, B7

The love child of Italian and Indian cooking, W's signature naan pizza is freshly baked in the tandoor oven and mouth-wateringly topped with everything from goat cheese to smoked salmon to guacamole. The wok curries and tortilla wraps are tasty too, while the spirulina-laced apple juice helps combat hangovers. (www.w-derimbiss.de; Kastanienallee 49; dishes €2-8; U-Bahn Rosenthaler Platz; M1, 12;)

Zula

ISRAELI €

9 | Map p114, D6

The humble garbanzo bean (chickpea) gets star treatment at this Israeli nosherie whose hummus is whipped up fresh daily and served with homemade pita bread. Enjoy it pure or with raw veggies, fried chicken or chilli con carne. (www.zula-berlin.com, in German; Husemannstrasse 10; mains €4-8; U-Bahn Eberswalder Strasse;)

The Dairy

INTERNATIONAL €

10 | Map p114, E4

There's certainly no shortage of bohemian daytime cafes in Prenzlauer Berg, but this hole-in-the-wall on Helmholtzplatz got our attention for its kick-ass coffee, granny-style baked goods, bulging sandwiches and intriguing daily blackboard specials: kangaroo stew or wild boar sandwich anyone? (www.thedairy.de; Raumerstrasse 12; dishes €3-6.50; 8am-6pm; U-Bahn Eberswalder Strasse; M1)

Schusterjunge

GERMAN €€

11 | Map p114, D4

This rustic corner joint doles out authentic Berlin charm with as much abandon as the German comfort cooking. Big platters of goulash, pork roast and *Sauerbraten* (vinegar-marinated beef pot roast) feed both tummy and soul, as do the regionally brewed Bürgerbräu and Bernauer Schwarzbier. (Danziger Strasse 9; mains €5-12; U-Bahn Eberswalder Strasse; M1)

Konnopke's Imbiss

GERMAN €

12 | Map p114, C4

This legendary sausage kitchen, now in modern digs but still oozing old-school charm below the elevated U-Bahn tracks, has been serving Currywurst, the quintessential Berlin snack, since 1930. Eat 'em while they're hot! (www.konnopke-imbiss.de; Schönhauser Allee 44b; sausage €1.30-1.70; 10am-8pm Mon-Fri, noon-8pm Sat; U-Bahn Eberswalder Strasse; M1, 12)

Drinking

Prater

BEER GARDEN

13 | Map p114, C5

Berlin's oldest beer garden (since 1837) has kept much of its traditional charm and is a fun spot for guzzling a cold one beneath the chestnut trees. Kids can romp around the small play area. (www.pratergarten.de; Kastanienallee 7-9; from noon Apr-Sep; U-Bahn Eberswalder Strasse; M1, 12)

Anna Blume
14 Map p114, E6   CAFE

Potent java, homemade cakes and flowers from the attached shop perfume the art nouveau interior of this corner cafe named for a Kurt Schwitters poem. In fine weather the big terrace is the perfect people-watching base. Great breakfast, too. (www.cafe-anna-blume.de; Kollwitzstrasse 83; ⏰8am-2am; U-Bahn Eberswalder Strasse; 🚋M1)

Becketts Kopf
15 Map p114, D3   COCKTAIL BAR

Beyond Samuel Beckett's head in the window, the art of cocktail-making is taken very seriously. In a sensuously lit, lushly designed setting, the barkeeps whip high-calibre spirits and freshly pressed juices into creative concoctions. (www.becketts-kopf.de; Pappelallee 64; ⏰from 8pm Tue-Sun; U-Bahn Eberswalder Strasse)

Kaffee Pakolat
16 Map p114, D3   CAFE

Flashback to the 19th century in this olde-worlde cafe-cum-store where the coffee is roasted on-site, the bread and cakes are made in the backroom bakery and the money is deposited in a ring-a-ding till from 1913. Antique furniture, enamel signs and sweet, unhurried service complete the illusion. Breakfast and snacks are available. (Raumerstrasse 40; ⏰10am-7pm Mon-Fri, to 6pm Sat & Sun; U-Bahn Eberswalder Strasse; 🚋M1, 12)

Deck 5
17 Map p114, D1   BEACH BAR

Soak up the city lights at this beach bar in the sky while sinking your toes into sand lugged to the rooftop of the Schönhauser Allee Arcaden shopping mall. Take the lift from within the mall or enter via a never-ending flight of stairs on Greifenhagener Strasse. (www.freiluftrebellen.de, in German; Schönhauser Allee 80; ⏰10am-midnight Apr-Sep; U-/S-Bahn Schönhauser Allee; 🚋M1)

Marietta
18 Map p114, D2   CAFE, BAR

Retro is now at this neighbourly self-service retreat where you can check out passing eye candy through the big window or lug your beverage to the dimly lit back room for quiet bantering. On Wednesday nights it's a launch pad for the local gay party circuit. (www.marietta-bar.de; Stargarder Strasse 13; ⏰from 10am; U-/S-Bahn Schönhauser Allee)

Bassy
19 Map p114, C8   CLUB

Most punters here have a post-Woodstock birth date but happily ride the retro wave at this trashy-charming den of darkness which plays only pre-1969 sounds. A burlesque show draws gawkers on Wednesdays, while drag diva Chantal hosts her 'House of Shame' gay parties on Thursdays. (www.bassy-club.de, in German; Schönhauser Allee 176a; ⏰Mon-Sat; U-Bahn Senefelderplatz)

Entertainment

Kulturbrauerei
CULTURAL CENTRE

20 ⭐ Map p114, C5

The fanciful red and yellow brick buildings of this 19th-century brewery are now a cultural powerhouse with a small village worth of venues, from concert and theatre halls to restaurants, nightclubs, galleries and a multiscreen cinema. (www.kulturbrauerei -berlin.de; Schönhauser Allee 36-39; U-Bahn Eberswalder Strasse)

Shopping

Erfinderladen Berlin
GIFTS, SOUVENIRS

21 🔒 Map p114, D4

Notepads for the shower, a toilet-paper holder made from vinyl records, an anti-monster spray for your kids – you never know what you're going to find in the Inventor Store, which is chock-full of items that are whimsical and bizarre but also stylish and practical. Check out the prototypes in the small museum in back. (www.erfinderladen-berlin.de, in German; Lychener Strasse 8; U-Bahn Eberswalder Strasse)

Flohmarkt am Arkonaplatz
FLEA MARKET

22 🔒 Map p114, A6

This small market lets you plug into the retro frenzy with plenty of groovy furniture, accessories, clothing, vinyl and books, including lots of GDR memorabilia. (Arkonaplatz; ⏰10am-5pm Sun; U-Bahn Bernauer Strasse)

Goldhahn & Sampson
FOOD

23 🔒 Map p114, E4

Pink Himalayan salt, Moroccan argan oil and crusty German breads are among the temptingly displayed delicacies at this posh food shop. Owners Sasha and Andreas hand-source all items, most of them rare, organic and from small suppliers. For inspiration, nose around the cookbook library or book a class at the on-site cooking school. (www.goldhahnundsampson.de; Dunckerstrasse 9; ⏰8am-8pm Mon-Fri, 10am-8pm Sat; U-Bahn Eberswalder Strasse)

Kollwitzplatz farmers market (p116)

Ta(u)sche
BAGS

24 🔒 Map p114, D4

Heike Braun and Antje Strubels, both landscape architects by training, are the masterminds behind these ingenious handmade messenger-style bags kitted out with exchangeable flaps that zip on and off in seconds. (www.tausche-berlin.de; Raumerstrasse 8; ⏱11am-8pm Mon-Fri, to 6pm Sat; U-Bahn Eberswalder Strasse)

Awear
FASHION

25 🔒 Map p114, B6

This trendy streetwear concept store feeds the urban-fashion craze with hats, hoodies, sneakers, tees and more by Nike, Sixpack France, Wood Wood, Just Female, CICO Copenhagen and plenty of other cool-hunter faves. (www.awear-berlin.de; Kastanienallee 75; ⏱noon-8pm Mon-Fri; U-Bahn Eberswalder Strasse; 🚊M1)

Luxus International
GIFTS, SOUVENIRS

26 🔒 Map p114, C5

There's no shortage of creative spirits in Berlin but few who can afford their own store. In comes Luxus International, which rents them a shelf or two to display everything from herbs-in-a-can and witty T-shirts to a Currywurst

card game and Trabi-embossed tote bags. (www.luxus-international.de; Kastanienallee 101; ⏱11am-8pm Mon-Sat, 1.30-7.30pm Sun; U-Bahn Eberswalder Strasse)

VEB Orange
VINTAGE

27 🔒 Map p114, B5

Viva retro! With its selection of the most beautiful things from the '60s and '70s, this place will remind you of how colourful, plastic and fun home decor used to be. There are all kinds of furnishings, accessories, lamps and fashions, much of it reflecting that irresistibly campy GDR spirit. (www.veborange.de; Oderberger Strasse 29; ⏱10am-8pm Mon-Sat; U-Bahn Eberswalder Strasse)

☑️ Top Tip

Shopping Areas

Aside from the Schönhauser Allee Arcaden mall by the eponymous U-/S-Bahn station (Map p114, D1), Prenzlauer Berg is mercifully devoid of chains. Streets where indie boutiques thrive include Kastanienallee and Oderberger Strasse, Stargarder Strasse and the streets around Helmholtzplatz. Most stores don't open until noon or later and close around 6pm or 7pm.

Explore

Kurfürstendamm

The glittering heart of West Berlin during the Cold War, Kurfürstendamm (aka Ku'damm) is now best known as Berlin's busiest shopping
strip, home to department stores, designer boutiques and high-street
chains. Venture off the boulevard to truly sample the area's bourgeois
charms as reflected in its palatial townhouses, distinctive shops, ritzy
restaurants and high-end entertainment venues.

The Sights in a Day

There will be a lot of walking today, so gather some strength with a bountiful breakfast at **Jules Verne** (p129), a darling neighbourhood cafe. Stroll over to Savignyplatz and down Grolmanstrasse to Kurfürstendamm and get the scoop on Berlin's tumultuous past at the **Story of Berlin** (p127). Follow up with an extended shopping spree down the boulevard, perhaps pausing to ponder the futility of war at the **Kaiser-Wilhelm-Gedächtniskirche** (pictured left; p126). Continue to the grand department store **KaDeWe** (p131), where you could have a late lunch in the glorious food hall.

Do a bit more shopping if you must, or make your way to the **Museum für Fotografie** (p126) to look at Helmut Newton's nudes and whatever else is on view. Now it's practically beer-o'clock and the tables in the **Dicke Wirtin** (p130) are singing their siren song.

A fine place for dinner is **Cafe im Literaturhaus** (p129) or, if you're a dedicated oenophile, **Enoteca Il Calice** (p127). Alternatively, catch a show and a bite in the stunning mirrored tent of **Bar Jeder Vernunft** (p130).

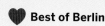 Best of Berlin

Bars
Puro Sky Lounge (p130)

Live Music
A-Trane (p131)

Cabaret & Performance
Bar Jeder Vernunft (p130)

Art
Käthe-Kollwitz-Museum (p126)

Museums
Museum für Fotografie (p126)

Story of Berlin (p127)

Shopping
KaDeWe (p131)

Getting There

Bus The M19, M29 and X10 travel along Kurfürstendamm.

S-Bahn Zoologischer Garten is the most central station.

U-Bahn Uhlandstrasse, Kurfürstendamm and Wittenbergplatz stations put you right into shopping central.

Goethestr

Steinplatz

Pestalozzistr

Grolmanstr

Knesebeckstr

Carmerstr

✖10

Kantstr

14 🚇

Savignyplatz

🚇16

20
🔒

✖11

Savignyplatz

Ⓢ

Kants

✖9

Leibnizstr

Wielandstr

Schlüterstr

Niebuhrstr

Bleibtreustr

CHARLOTTENBURG

Knesebeckstr

Grolmanstr

Uhlandstr

Mommsenstr

Uhlandstr

7
✖

Walter-Benjamin-
Platz

George-
Grosz-Platz

Kurfürstendamm

Uhlandstr

🔒15

8🔒

🔒22

2◉
**Käthe-Kollwitz-
Museum**

4
◉
*Story of
Berlin*

Konstanzer Str

Olivaer
Platz

Xantener Str

Lietzenburger Str

✖12

Pfalzburger Str

Fasanenp

Bayerische Str

Württembergische Str

Pariser Str

Sächsische Str

Emser Str

Ludwigkirchplatz

Ludwigkirchstr

Pariser Str

E

F

G

H

Museum für
Fotografie **3** ⊚

Hardenbergstr

Jebenstr

⊛ Zoologischer
Garten
Hardenbergplatz

Ⓢ
Zoologischer
Garten

Ⓤ Zoologischer
Garten

▲ 0
Ⓝ   0

0   200 m
0.1 miles

Zoologischer
Garten

1

Zoo
Berlin ⊚ **5**

Zoo
Aquarium
Berlin ⊚ **6**

Olof-
Palme-Platz

**Budapester
Str**

Budapester Str

Kurfürstenstr

Breitscheidplatz

Kaiser-Wilhelm- ⊚ **1**
Gedächtniskirche

ⓘ

Ⓤ Kurfürstendamm

Europa
Center ⚲
13

Tauentzienstr

Ansbacher Str

3

Meinekestr

Joachimstaler Str

Los-
Angeles-
Platz

Marburger Str

Nürnberger Str

🔒
19

Ⓤ
Wittenbergplatz

4

Rankeplatz

Rankestr

Eisleberner Str

Augsburger ⊚
Str

Ⓤ
Augsburger Str

Lietzenburger Str

Nürnberger
Platz

An der Urania
Lietzenburger Str

Fuggerstr

Schaperstr

Bamberger Str

Ansbacher Str

Welserstr

5

17

Geisbergstr

Sights

Kaiser-Wilhelm-Gedächtniskirche   CHURCH

1 ⊙ Map p124, G2

The bombed-out tower of this landmark church serves as an anti-war memorial, standing quiet and dignified amid the roaring traffic. The 1895 original was a real beauty, as you can tell from the before and after pictures on the ground floor. The adjacent octagonal hall of worship, added in 1961, has amazing midnight-blue glass walls and a giant 'floating' Jesus. (Emperor William Memorial Church; www.gedaechtniskirche-berlin.de; Breitscheidplatz; ⊙9am-7pm; U-Bahn Kurfürstendamm)

Käthe-Kollwitz-Museum   MUSEUM

2 ⊙ Map p124, D4

This exquisite museum trains the spotlight on Käthe Kollwitz, one of the top German female artists, whose social and political awareness lent a tortured power to her work. After losing both her son and grandson on the battlefields of Europe, death and motherhood became recurring themes. (www.kaethe-kollwitz.de; Fasanenstrasse 24; adult/concession €6/3; ⊙11am-6pm; U-Bahn Uhlandstrasse)

Museum für Fotografie   MUSEUM

3 ⊙ Map p124, F1

The photographic legacy of Helmut Newton, the Berlin-born *enfant terrible* of fashion and lifestyle photography, forms the core of this museum in a former Prussian officers' casino behind Zoologischer Garten. On the top floor, the gloriously restored barrel-vaulted **Kaisersaal** (Emperor's Hall) forms a grand backdrop for high-calibre changing photography exhibits. (Museum of Photography; www.smb.museum; Jebensstrasse 2; adult/concession incl same-day admission to Sammlung Scharf-Gerstenberg €8/4;

Understand

Käthe Kollwitz

Käthe Kollwitz (1867–1945) was the superstar among 20th-century female German artists, although she herself would probably frown at such a label. Modest, selfless and empathetic, Kollwitz is best known for her deeply moving, often heart-wrenching woodcuts, sculptures and lithographs that profoundly capture the depth of human hardship, suffering and sorrow. Her art was greatly influenced by the despair and poverty she observed in Berlin's working-class ghettos and by the deaths of her son in the battlefields of WWI and of her grandson in WWII. A member of the Berlin Secession, Kollwitz was the first female professor at the prestigious Prussian Academy of Arts until the Nazis forced her to resign in 1933. She died of natural causes in 1945.

⏱10am-6pm Tue, Wed & Fri-Sun, to 10pm Thu;
U-/S-Bahn Zoologischer Garten)

Story of Berlin　MUSEUM

4 ⊚ Map p124, C4

This multimedia museum breaks down
800 years of Berlin history into bite-
sized chunks, from the city's founding
in 1237 to the fall of the Berlin Wall. A
highlight is a tour of a fully functional
Cold War–era atomic bunker beneath
the building. Enter through the
shopping mall. (www.story-of-berlin.de;
Kurfürstendamm 207-208; adult/concession
€10/8; ⏱10am-8pm, last admission & bunker
tour 6pm; U-Bahn Uhlandstrasse)

Zoo Berlin　ZOO

5 ⊚ Map p124, G2

Germany's oldest animal park opened
in 1844 with furry and feathered
critters from the royal family's private
reserve. Today some 16,000 animals
from all continents, 1500 species in
total, make their home here. Cheeky
orang-utans, cuddly koalas, endan-
gered rhinos, playful penguins and
Bao Bao, a rare giant panda, are
among the biggest celebrities. (www.
zoo-berlin.de; Hardenbergplatz 8; adult/child
€13/6.50; ⏱9am-7pm mid-Mar–mid-Sep,
9am-5pm mid-Sep–mid-Mar; U-/S-Bahn
Zoologischer Garten)

Zoo Aquarium Berlin　AQUARIUM

6 ⊚ Map p124, H2

Three floors of exotic fish, amphibians
and reptiles await at this endearingly
old-fashioned aquarium with its dark-

Zoo Berlin

ened halls and glowing tanks. Some of
the specimens in the famous Crocodile
Hall could be the stuff of nightmares,
but dancing jellyfish, iridescent
poison frogs and a real-life 'Nemo'
should bring smiles to even the most
Playstation-jaded youngsters. (www
.aquarium-berlin.de; Budapester Strasse 32;
adult/child €13/6.50; ⏱9am-6pm; U-/S-Bahn
Zoologischer Garten)

Eating

Enoteca Il Calice　ITALIAN €€€

7 ✗ Map p124, A3

Superb wines from all regions of 'the
Boot' flow as freely as the conversation at this elegant Italian outpost.

MARTIN MOOS/LONELY PLANET IMAGES ©

Understand
Berlin in the 'Golden' Twenties

The 1920s began as anything but golden, marked by a lost war, social and political instability, hyperinflation, hunger and disease. Many Berliners responded like there was no tomorrow and made their city as much a den of decadence as a cauldron of creativity. Cabaret, Dada and jazz flourished. Pleasure pits popped up everywhere, turning the city into a 'sextropolis' of Dionysian dimensions. Bursting with energy, it became a laboratory for anything new and modern, drawing giants of architecture (Hans Scharoun, Walter Gropius), fine arts (George Grosz, Max Beckmann) and literature (Bertolt Brecht, Christopher Isherwood).

Cafes & Cabaret
Cabarets provided a titillating fantasy of play and display where transvestites, singers, magicians, dancers and other entertainers made audiences forget about the harsh realities. Kurfürstendamm evolved into a major nightlife hub with glamorous cinemas, theatres and restaurants. The Romanisches Café, on the site of today's Europa Center, was practically the second living room for artists, actors, writers, photographers, film producers and other creative types, some famous, most not. German writer Erich Kästner even called it the 'waiting room of the talented'.

Celluloid History
The 1920s and early '30s were also a boom time for Berlin cinema, with Marlene Dietrich seducing the world and the mighty UFA studio producing virtually all of Germany's celluloid output. Fritz Lang, whose seminal works *Metropolis* (1926) and *M* (1931) brought him international fame, was among dominant filmmakers.

The Crash
The fun came to an instant end when the US stock market crashed in 1929, plunging the world into economic depression. Within weeks, half a million Berliners were jobless and riots and demonstrations again ruled the streets. The volatile, increasingly polarised political climate led to clashes between communists and the emerging NSDAP, led by Adolf Hitler. Soon jackboots, Brownshirts, oppression and fear would dominate daily life in Germany.

Resist the temptation to make a meal of the antipasti alone and test the chef's considerable talents with such seasonally calibrated concoctions as coffee-oil poached sturgeon or air-dried mullet roe pasta. (☎324 2308; www.ilcalice.de; Walter-Benjamin-Platz 4; mains €13-34; ☺lunch Mon-Sat, dinner nightly; U-Bahn Adenauerplatz)

Café-Restaurant Wintergarten im Literaturhaus
INTERNATIONAL €€

8 🍴 Map p124, D3

The hustle and bustle of Ku'damm is only a stone's throw away from this genteel art nouveau villa with attached bookstore. Tuck into seasonal bistro cuisine amid elegant Old Berlin flair in the gracefully stucco-ornamented rooms or, if weather permits, the idyllic garden. Breakfast until 2pm. (www.literaturhaus-berlin.de, in German; Fasanenstrasse 23; mains €8-16; ☺9.30am-1am; U-Bahn Uhlandstrasse; 🍴)

Brel
BELGIAN €€

9 🍴 Map p124, C2

Belgian cult crooner Jacques Brel is the namesake of this corner bistro in a former bordello that now draws bleary-eyed bohos for coffee and croissants, suits and tourists for €9 lunches, and Francophile couples for frog legs, steaks and snails at dinnertime. Breakfast until 6pm. (www.cafebrel.de, in German; Savignyplatz 1; mains €11-21; ☺9am-1am; S-Bahn Savignyplatz)

Good Friends
CHINESE €€

10 🍴 Map p124, B2

Sinophiles tired of the Kung Pao school of Chinese cooking will appreciate the real thing at this well-established Cantonese restaurant. The ducks dangling in the window are the overture to a menu long enough to confuse Confucius. If jellyfish with eggs or fried pork belly sound too much like a *Survivor* challenge, you can always fall back on, well, Kung Pao chicken. (www.goodfriends-berlin.de; Kantstrasse 30; mains €10-20; S-Bahn Savignyplatz)

Jules Verne
INTERNATIONAL €€

11 🍴 Map p124, B2

Jules Verne was a well-travelled man, so it's only fitting that a cafe bearing his name would feature a globetrotting menu. French oysters, Austrian schnitzel and Moroccan couscous are all perennial bestsellers. (☎3180 9410; www.jules-verne-berlin.de, in German; Schlüterstrasse 61; dinner mains €11-25; ☺9am-1am; S-Bahn Savignyplatz; 🍴)

🔍 Local Life
Berlin's 'Little Asia'
It's not quite Chinatown, but if you're in the mood for Asian food simply head to **Kantstrasse** (Map p124, A2-C2) between Savignyplatz and Wilmersdorfer Strasse, which has the city's greatest concentration of Chinese, Vietnamese, Thai and Japanese restaurants, shops and soup kitchens. At lunchtime, most offer value-priced lunch specials.

Mr Hai Kabuki
JAPANESE €€€

12 Map p124, B4

Yes, it does have classic nigiri and maki but most regulars flock to Mr Hai for more unconventional sushi morsels, composed like little works of art. Some creations feature kimchi, pumpkin and cream, others are flambéed and deep-fried. Sounds bizarre, but it works. (☎ 8862 8136; www.mrhai .de; Olivaer Platz 10; platters €12-22; U-Bahn Adenauerplatz)

Drinking

Puro Sky Lounge
BAR, CLUB

13 Map p124, G3

Puro has quite literally raised the bar in Charlottenburg – by moving it to the 20th floor of the Europa Center. Trade Berlin funky-trash for sleek decor, fabulous views and high-heeled hotties. (www.puro-berlin.de, in German; Tauentzienstrasse 11; ☺Tue-Sat; U-Bahn Kurfürstendamm)

Zwiebelfisch
BAR

14 Map p124, C2

With its clientele of grizzled and aspiring artists, actors and writers, this cosy pub has been Charlottenburg at its boho best since the patchouli-perfumed 1960s. Everyone's a little older these days, but it's still a great place for guzzling that final drink while the iPad crowd is gearing up for another day at the office. (www

.zwiebelfisch-berlin.de, in German; Savignyplatz 5; ☺noon-6am; S-Bahn Savignyplatz)

Berliner Kaffeerösterei
CAFE

15 Map p124, D3

Move over Starbucks. Berlin's best coffee hails from this old-fashioned outfit whose java-meisters scour the world for the cream of the bean crop and then roast them to perfection on-site. Yummy cakes to boot. (www .berliner-kaffeeroesterei.de; Uhlandstrasse 173-174; U-Bahn Uhlandstrasse)

Dicke Wirtin
PUB

16 Map p124, C2

Old Berlin charm oozes from every nook and cranny of this old-timey pub, which pours eight draught beers (including the superb Kloster Andechs) and nearly three dozen homemade schnapps varieties. Hearty local fare keeps brains balanced. (www .dicke-wirtin.de; Carmerstrasse 9; ☺from noon; S-Bahn Savignyplatz)

Entertainment

Bar jeder Vernunft
CABARET

17 Map p124, E5

Life's still a cabaret at this intimate 1912 art nouveau mirrored tent, which puts on song-and-dance shows, comedy and variety acts. Enter via the parking lot. (☎ 883 1582; www.bar-jeder -vernunft.de; Schaperstrasse 24; U-Bahn Spichernstrasse)

A-Trane

JAZZ

18 ⭐ Map p124, C1

Herbie Hancock and Diana Krall have anointed the stage of this intimate jazz club, but mostly it's emerging talent bringing their A-game to the A-Trane. Entry is free on Monday when local boy Andreas Schmidt shows off his skills, and after 12.30am on Saturday for the late-night jam session. (www.a-trane.de, in German; Bleibtreustrasse 1; ⊙ daily; S-Bahn Savignyplatz)

Shopping

KaDeWe

DEPARTMENT STORE

19 🔒 Map p124, H4

Just past the centennial mark, this venerable department store is so massive that a pirate-style campaign is the best way to plunder its bounty. If pushed for time, at least hurry up to the legendary gourmet food hall on the 6th floor. (www.kadewe-berlin.de; Tauentzienstrasse 21-24; U-Bahn Wittenbergplatz)

Stilwerk

INTERIOR DESIGN

20 🔒 Map p124, D2

If this four-floor temple of good taste doesn't get your decorative juices flowing, nothing will. Everything for home and hearth is here – towels to mattresses – all by such top names as Bang & Olufsen, Möve, BoConcept, ligne roset et al. (www.stilwerk.de, in German; Kantstrasse 17; S-Bahn Savignyplatz)

🔍 Local Life
Shop 'til You Drop

Charlottenburg's shopping spine is Kurfürstendamm and its eastern extension, Tauentzienstrasse. Kantstrasse, meanwhile, is the go-to zone for home designs. Connecting side streets such as Bleibtreustrasse and Fasanenstrasse house upscale indie and designer boutiques, bookstores and galleries.

Steiff in Berlin

TOYS

21 🔒 Map p124, E3

The cuddly creations of this famous stuffed-animal company, founded in 1880 by Margarete Steiff (who in 1902 invented the teddy bear – named for US president Teddy Roosevelt, whom she admired), are tailor-made for snuggles. The fluffy menagerie (including limited-edition collectibles) at this flagship store will have all ages feeling warm and fuzzy. (www.steiff.de; Kurfürstendamm 220; U-Bahn Uhlandstrasse)

Hautnah

EROTICA

22 🔒 Map p124, D4

Those who worship at the altar of hedonism should check out this three-floor emporium of erotica. Fetishistas can stock up on latex bustiers, rubber bodysuits, sex toys, themed get-ups and vertiginous footwear. Wine cellar in the basement. (www.hautnahberlin.de, in German; Uhlandstrasse 170; ⊙ noon-8pm Mon-Fri, 11am-4pm Sat; S-Bahn Uhlandstrasse)

Local Life
Exploring Many-Sided Schöneberg

Getting There

Schöneberg is wedged between Kurfürsten-damm and Kreuzberg.

U-Bahn This itinerary is bookended by two stations: Viktoria-Luise-Platz (U4) and Kleistpark (U7).

Schöneberg flaunts a mellow middle-class identity but has a radical pedigree rooted in the squatter days of the '80s. Its multifaceted character nicely unfolds as you stroll from bourgeois Viktoria-Luise-Platz through Berlin's original gay quarter and along streets squeezed tight with boho cafes and well-edited indie boutiques to ethnically flavoured Hauptstrasse.

❶ Viktoria-Luise-Platz

Soak up the laid-back vibe of Schöneberg's prettiest square, a classic symphony of towering trees, a sprightly fountain and benches where locals swap gossip, catch up on reading or watch kids at play. Surrounding the square are several cafes and ornate historic facades at numbers 7, 12 and 12a.

❷ Gay Village

The rainbow flags above bars and stores on Motzstrasse signal that you're now in the heart of Berlin's original gay area. A memorial plaque at the south entrance of Nollendorfplatz U-Bahn station commemorates homosexual victims of the Nazi era.

❸ Coffee at Cafe Berio

Unchanged-in-decades **Cafe Berio** (www.cafeberio.de; Maassenstrasse 7; ⏱from 7am Mon-Fri, 8am Sat & Sun) is a lone hold-out among the identikit 'lounge-restaurants' that have invaded Maassenstrasse. Here you can still get an honest cappuccino and nibble sweet cakes, preferably from a perch on the pavement terrace. A gay fave.

❹ Farmers Market

If it's Wednesday or Saturday morning, you're in luck because ho-hum Winterfeldtplatz erupts with farm-fresh fare. Along with seasonal produce you'll find handmade cheeses, cured meats, olives, local honey and plenty more staples and surprises. Saturday also has artsy-craftsy stalls.

❺ Chocophile Alert

Winterfeldt Schokoladen (www.winterfeldt-schokoladen.de; Goltzstrasse 23; ⏱9am-8pm Mon-Fri, to 6pm Sat) stocks a vast range of international handmade gourmet chocolates, all displayed gallery-style in the original oak fixtures of a 19th-century pharmacy. Try a cup of decadent hot chocolate.

❻ Shopping on Goltzstrasse

Goltzstrasse is choc-a-block with indie boutiques selling everything from vintage clothing to slinky underwear, antique books to handmade jewellery, exotic teas to cooking supplies. No high-street chain in sight! Wedged in between are comfy cafes and casual eateries.

❼ Double Eye

Local coffee lovers are addicted to the award-winning espresso drinks of **Double Eye** (Akazienstrasse 22; ⏱8.47am-6.29pm Mon-Fri, 9.01am-5.57pm Sat), which is why no one minds the queue that usually snakes right out the door. Prices are low, smiles big and the quality tops.

❽ Hauptstrasse

Boutiques gradually give way to grocers and cafes dishing up doner kebab. The main artery of this multiculti section of Schöneberg is bustling Hauptstrasse, home to **Öz-Gida** at number 16, a Turkish supermarket known citywide for its olive selection, cheese spreads and quality meats. David Bowie used to live at Hauptstrasse 155.

Top Sights
Schloss Charlottenburg

Getting There

Schloss Charlottenburg is 3km northwest of Zoologischer Garten.

U-Bahn From Sophie-Charlotte-Platz (U2) station it's a scenic 1km walk via Schlossstrasse or a ride on bus 309.

Charlottenburg Palace is the largest and most beautiful of Berlin's remaining nine royal residences. More than any other, it still reflects the one-time grandeur of the Hohenzollern clan, which ruled the region from 1415 until 1918. Originally a petite summer retreat, the palace grew into an exquisite baroque pile and is a wonderful place to spend a day, especially in summer when you can fold a stroll or a picnic in the lush gardens into a day of peeking at royal treasures.

Don't Miss

Altes Schloss

The original royal living quarters in the baroque **Old Palace** (adult/concession €12/8; ⏲10am-6pm Tue-Sun Apr-Oct, to 5pm Nov-Mar) are an extravaganza in stucco, brocade and overall opulence. Admire family portraits in the Oak Gallery, the charming Oval Hall overlooking the gardens, Chinese and Japanese blueware in the Porcelain Chamber, and the Eosander Chapel with its *trompe l'œil* arches.

Neuer Flügel

Added under Frederick the Great in 1746, the **New Wing** (adult/concession €6/5; ⏲10am-6pm Wed-Mon Apr-Oct, to 5pm Nov-Mar) contains the palace's most beautiful rooms, including the confection-like White Hall banquet room and the Golden Gallery, a rococo fantasy of mirrors and gilding. The Concert Room has a prized collection of paintings by French masters.

Schlossgarten

The expansive baroque gardens linking the palace and the Spree River are part formal French, part unruly English and all idyllic playground. Wandering around the shady paths, lawns and carp pond, you'll eventually stumble upon the sombre Mausoleum and the charming Belvedere.

Belvedere

This pint-size late-rococo **palace** (adult/concession €3/2.50; ⏲10am-6pm Tue-Sun Apr-Oct, noon-4pm Sat & Sun Nov-Mar), built in 1788 by Carl Gotthard Langhans as a teahouse for King Friedrich Wilhelm II, today makes an elegant setting for porcelain masterpieces by the royal manufacturer KPM. Lavish dinnerware services and dainty teacups from the time of Napoleon are among the highlights.

📞320 911

www.spsg.de

Spandauer Damm

admission see individual entries; day pass adult/concession €14/10

⏲see individual entries

☑ Top Tips

▶ Arrive early to avoid long queues on weekends and in summer.

▶ Visit Wednesday to Sunday, when all palace buildings are open.

▶ The day pass is good for admission to all buildings except the Neuer Flügel.

▶ A visit of the palace is easily combined with a spin around the trio of adjacent art museums.

✗ Take a Break

▶ Near the park entrance, the **Kleine Orangerie** (www.kleine orangerie.de; mains €6-15) serves breakfast, snacks, meals and cakes.

▶ In fine weather, pack a picnic.

Understand
Palace Planning

The lavish Schloss Charlottenburg you see today started out rather modestly as the summer retreat of Sophie-Charlotte, wife of Elector Friedrich III (1657–1713). Arnold Nering drew up the initial plans, which were expanded in the mode of Versailles by Johann Friedrich Eosander after the elector was elevated to King Friedrich I in 1701. Subsequent royals dabbled with the compound, most notably Frederick the Great who added the spectacular Neuer Flügel (New Wing). The Neuer Pavillon and the Mausoleum and Belvedere in the palace gardens date to the 19th century.

Neuer Pavillon

This Karl Friedrich Schinkel–designed **mini-palace** (adult/concession €4/3; ⏲10am-6pm Tue-Sun Apr-Oct, noon-4pm Nov-Mar) was originally a summer retreat of King Friedrich Wilhelm III. Modelled on an Italian villa where the king had stayed, it displays paintings from the Romantic and Biedermeier periods alongside furniture, sculpture, porcelain and other period items.

Mausoleum

The neoclassical 1815 **Mausoleum** (admission free; ⏲10am-6pm Tue-Sun Apr-Oct) was conceived as the resting place of the much-beloved Queen Luise. Its fancy marble sarcophagi are now the final pad of not just her but other bigshot royals, including Luise's husband King Friedrich III and Emperor William I and his wife Augusta.

Nearby: Sammlung Scharf-Gerstenberg

Across the street from the main palace entrance, this stellar **gallery** (www.smb.museum; Schlossstrasse 70; adult/concession €6/3; ⏲10am-6pm Tue-Sun) showcases surrealist art by René Magritte and Max Ernst alongside dreamscapes by Salvador Dalí and Jean Dubuffet. Standouts among their 18th-century forerunners include Francisco Goya's spooky etchings and the creepy dungeon scenes by Giovanni Battista Piranesi.

Nearby: Bröhan Museum

This fine **museum** (www.broehan-museum.de; Schlossstrasse 1a; adult/concession €6/4; ⏲10am-6pm Tue-Sun) trains the spotlight on art nouveau, art deco and functionalism, decorative styles in vogue between 1889 and 1939. Highlights include period rooms by Hector Guimard and Peter Behrens, a Berlin Secession picture gallery, and an entire floor dedicated to Henry van de Velde.

Nearby: Museum Berggruen

Fans of Pablo Picasso, Paul Klee, Henri Matisse and Alberto Giacometti will be in their element at this **museum** (www.smb.museum; Schlossstrasse 1), which is undergoing extensive expansion. At press time, the reopening was scheduled for summer 2012.

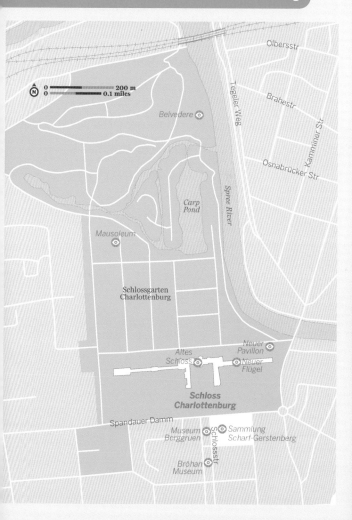

N

0 ——————— 200 m
0 ——————— 0.1 miles

Olbersstr

Brahestr

Belvedere

Tegeler Weg

Kamminer Str

Osnabrücker Str

Carp
Pond

Spree River

Mausoleum

Schlossgarten
Charlottenburg

Neuer
Pavillon

Altes
Schloss

Neuer
Flügel

Schloss
Charlottenburg

Spandauer Damm

Museum
Berggruen

Sammlung
Scharf-Gerstenberg

Schlossstr

Bröhan
Museum

Top Sights
Schloss & Park Sanssouci

Getting There

Sanssouci is 24km southwest of the city centre. You need a transport ticket covering zones A, B and C (€3).

S-Bahn The S7 makes the trip from central Berlin in about 40 minutes.

This glorious park-and-palace ensemble is what happens when a king has good taste, plenty of cash and access to the finest architects and artists of the day. A quick train ride from Berlin, in Potsdam, Sanssouci was dreamed up by Frederick the Great (1712–86) and is anchored by the eponymous palace, built as a summer retreat. His great-great-nephew Friedrich Wilhelm IV (1795–1861) added a few more buildings. Unesco gave the entire thing World Heritage status in 1990.

Don't Miss

Schloss Sanssouci

This rococo jewel of a **palace** (adult/concession €12/8 Apr-Oct, €8/5 Nov-Mar; ⊙10am-6pm Tue-Sun Apr-Oct, to 5pm Nov-Mar) sits above vine-draped terraces with Frederick the Great's grave nearby. Standouts on the audioguided tours include the whimsically decorated concert hall, where the king himself gave flute recitals, and the domed Marble Hall modelled after the Pantheon in Rome.

Bibliothek

None of the rooms in Schloss Sanssouci reflect Frederick's penchant for privacy as much as his intimate library lidded by a gilded sunburst ceiling. Here the 'philosopher king' would find solace surrounded by more than 2000 leather-bound tomes ranging from ancient Greek poetry to the latest releases by his friend Voltaire.

Chinesisches Haus

The Far East was all the rage in the 18th century, as reflected in the adorable **Chinese House** (admission €2; ⊙10am-6pm Tue-Sun May-Oct). The cloverleaf-shaped pavilion is among the park's most photographed buildings, thanks to an enchanting exterior of exotically dressed gilded figures sipping tea, dancing and playing musical instruments. Inside is a precious porcelain collection.

Bildergalerie

Adjacent to Schloss Sanssouci, the **Picture Gallery** (adult/concession €3/2.50; ⊙10am-5pm Tue-Sun May-Oct) is the oldest royal museum in Germany, resplendent in yellow and white marble and elaborate stuccowork. It shelters Frederick's collection of Old Masters, including such pearls as Caravaggio's *Doubting Thomas,* Anton van Dyck's *Pentecost* and several works by Peter Paul Rubens.

---

www.spsg.de

admission see individual entries; day pass adult/concession €19/14

⊙see individual entries; park open dawn to dusk

☑ Top Tips

▶ For information, pop by the **Sanssouci Visitor Center** (An der Orangerie 1; ⊙8.30am-5pm Apr-Oct, 9am-4pm Nov-Mar).

▶ For guaranteed admission join the **Potsdam Sanssouci Tour** (www .potsdam-tourismus.de). Otherwise arrive early and avoid weekends and holidays.

▶ Most buildings are closed on Mondays.

✕ Take a Break

For coffee, cake and regional cuisine, stop by the **Drachenhaus** (mains €14-18).

The huge **Potsdam Historische Mühle** (mains €10-18; ⊙8am-11pm) lures punters with international favourites, a beer garden and a children's playground.

Neues Palais

The **New Palace** (adult/concession €6/5; ⊙10am-6pm Wed-Mon Apr-Oct, to 5pm Nov-Mar) has made-to-impress dimensions, a central dome and a lavish exterior capped with a parade of sandstone figures. It was the final palace built by Frederick the Great, primarily for representational purposes. Only the last German Kaiser, Wilhelm II, actually used it as a residence (until 1918).

Grottensaal

The most impressive room visited on tours of the New Palace is the **Grotto Hall**, a rococo marble-and-glass delight. Completely covered in a mosaic of shells, fossils, minerals, snails and semiprecious stones, it once provided access to the royal apartments.

Orangerie

The 300m-long Mediterranean-styled **Orangery** (adult/concession €4/3; ⊙10am-6pm Tue-Sun May-Oct, weekends only Apr) was Friedrich Wilhelm IV's favourite building project and reflects his love for all things Italian. Tours take in the **Raphaelsaal**, which brims with 19th-century copies of the famous painter's masterpieces, while the **tower** (€2) delivers sweeping park views.

Belvedere auf dem Klausberg

From the Orangery, a tree-lined path forms a visual axis to this temple-like **pavilion** (admission €2; ⊙10am-6pm Sat & Sun May-Oct), modelled on Nero's palace in Rome. Views from the two-storey columned round building take in the park, the surrounds and the city of

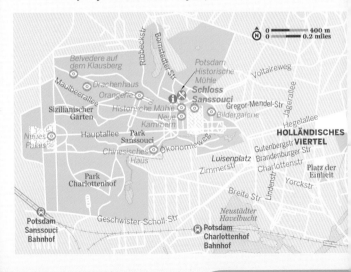

Potsdam. The sumptuous interior was recently restored following WWII damage.

Drachenhaus

En route to the Belvedere, you'll pass the exotic Dragon House, a Chinese miniature palace built in 1770. Inspired by the Ta-Ho pagoda in Canton, it is guarded by an entire army of dragons and now houses a pleasant cafe-restaurant.

Neue Kammern

The **New Chambers** (adult/concession €4/3; ⊙10am-6pm Tue-Sun May-Oct, limited hours in winter) was originally an orangery and later converted into a guesthouse. The interior drips in opulence, most notably in the Ovidsaal, a grand ballroom with gilded reliefs depicting scenes from *Metamorphosis,* and in the Jasper Hall, drenched in precious stones and topped by a ceiling fresco starring Venus.

Park Charlottenhof

Laid out by Peter Lenné for Friedrich Wilhelm IV, this park segues from Park Sanssouci but gets much fewer visitors. Buildings in this quiet corner bear the stamp of Karl Friedrich Schinkel, most notably the neoclassical **Schloss Charlottenhof** (currently closed) and the nearby **Roman Baths** (adult/concession €3/2.50; ⊙10am-6pm Tue-Sun May-Oct), a picturesque ensemble of Italian country villas.

Historische Mühle

This is a functioning replica of the palace's original Dutch-style 18th-century **windmill** (adult/child €3/2; ⊙10am-6pm daily Apr-Oct, 10am-4pm Sat & Sun Nov & Jan-Mar). There's a shop on the ground floor, three exhibit floors detailing mill technology and a top-floor viewing platform.

Nearby: Holländisches Viertel

To get a sense of Potsdam beyond the palace, head east for about 1km via the pedestrianised Brandenburger Strasse shopping strip to the **Dutch Quarter**. This compact neighbourhood of gabled red-brick houses was built around 1730 for Dutch workers invited by Friedrich Wilhelm I. It's now home to cafes, restaurants, boutiques and galleries. Mittelstrasse is especially scenic.

The Best of
Berlin

Berlin's Best Walks

Berlin's Best...

Spree River near the Bodemuseum
JEAN-PIERRE LESCOURRET/LONELY PLANET IMAGES ©

Best Walks
Historical Highlights

🏃 The Walk

This walk checks off Berlin's blockbuster landmarks as it cuts right through the historic city centre called Mitte (literally 'Middle'). This is the birthplace and glamorous heart of Berlin, a high-octane cocktail of culture, architecture and commerce. You'll follow in the footsteps of kings and soldiers, marvel at grand architecture and stroll humble cobbled lanes, travel from the Middle Ages to the future and be awed by some of the world's finest works of art. Bring that camera!

Start Reichstag; U-Bahn Bundestag; 🚌100, TXL

Finish Hackescher Markt; S-Bahn Hackescher Markt

Length 4.5km; 1½ to two hours

✕ Take a Break

Along Unter den Linden, **Cafe Einstein** (www .einsteinudl.de; Unter den Linden 42; mains €9-18; ⏱7am-10pm) makes for an arty pit stop.

View of the Nikolaiviertel from the Spree River

❶ Reichstag

The 1894 **Reichstag** (p24) is the historic anchor of Berlin's federal government quarter. The sparkling glass dome, added during the building's 1990s revamp, has become a shining beacon of unified Berlin.

❷ Brandenburg Gate

The only remaining gate of Berlin's 18th-century town wall, the **Brandenburg Gate** (p26) became an involuntary neighbour of the Berlin Wall during the Cold War. It's now a cheery symbol of German reunification.

❸ Unter den Linden

Originally a riding path linking the city palace with the royal hunting grounds in Tiergarten, **Unter den Linden** has been Berlin's showpiece road since the 18th century. Grand old buildings line up like Prussian soldiers for inspection, including the city's oldest university and the Staatsoper opera house.

④ Gendarmenmarkt

Berlin's most beautiful square, **Gendarmenmarkt** (p32) is bookended by domed cathedrals with the famous Konzerthaus (Concert Hall) in between. Streets around here are lined with elegant hotels, upmarket restaurants and fancy cocktail bars.

⑤ Museum Island

The sculpture-studded Palace Bridge leads to the twee Spree island where Berlin's settlement began in the 13th century. Its northern half, **Museum Island** (p40) is a Unesco-recognised treasure chest of art, sculpture and objects spread across five grand museums.

⑥ Nikolaiviertel

With its cobbled lanes and higgledy-piggledy houses, the **Nikolai Quarter** may look medieval but don't be fooled: it's a product of the 1980s, built by the GDR government to celebrate Berlin's 750th birthday. A stand-out among the few original buildings is the twin-spired Nikolaikirche (Church of St Nicholas), now a museum.

⑦ Scheunenviertel

Berlin's historic Jewish Quarter, the **Scheunenviertel** languished in GDR days but, since reunification, has been rebooted as a charismatic shopping, eating and partying zone. Fuel up on coffee at the Hackesche Höfe courtyard complex, then schlep to the many indie boutiques for local fashions, edgy art and clever knick-knacks.

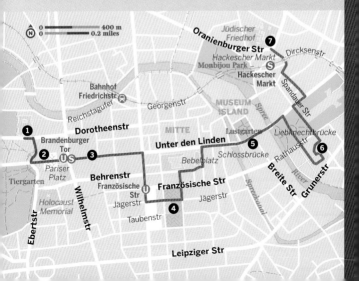

Best Walks
Walking the Wall

🏃 The Walk

Construction of the Berlin Wall began shortly after midnight on 13 August 1961. For the next 28 years this grim barrier divided a city and its people, becoming the most visible symbol of the Cold War. By now the two city halves have visually merged so perfectly that it takes a keen eye to tell East from West. To give you a sense of the period of division, this walk follows the most central section of the Berlin Wall. For a more in-depth experience, rent the multimedia **Mauerguide** (WallGuide; www.mauer guide.com; per day €10) at Checkpoint Charlie.

Start Checkpoint Charlie; U-Bahn Kochstrasse

Finish Parlament der Bäume; U-Bahn Bundestag

Length 3km; one hour

🍴 Take a Break

Potsdamer Platz (p66) has the biggest concentration of eating and drinking options.

Sections of the Berlin Wall preserved in Potsdamer Platz

❶ Checkpoint Charlie

As the third Allied checkpoint, **Checkpoint Charlie** (p63) got its name from the third letter in the NATO phonetic alphabet. Weeks after the Wall was built, US and Soviet tanks faced off here in one of the tensest moments of the Cold War.

❷ Niederkirchner Strasse

Along **Niederkirchner Strasse** looms a 200m-long section of the original outer border wall. Scarred by souvenir hunters, it's now protected by a fence. The border strip was very narrow here, with the inner wall abutting such buildings as the former Nazi Air Force Ministry.

❸ Watchtower

This is one of the few remaining GDR **border watchtowers**. Guards had to climb up a slim round shaft to reach the octagonal observation perch. Introduced in 1969, this cramped model was later replaced by larger square towers.

4 Potsdamer Platz

Potsdamer Platz used to be a massive no-man's-land bisected by the Berlin Wall and a 'death strip' several hundred metres wide. Outside the northern S-Bahn station entrance are a few **Berlin Wall segments** with panels pointing to other Wall memorial sites and future Wall-related projects.

5 Brandenburg Gate

The **Brandenburg Gate** (p26) was where

construction of the Wall began. Many statesmen gave speeches in front of it, perhaps most famously former US president Ronald Reagan who, in 1987, uttered the words: 'Mr Gorbachev – tear down this wall!'. Two years later, the Wall was history.

6 Art Installation

On the riverwalk level of the Marie-Elisabeth-Lüders-Haus, which houses the parliamentary library, an **art installation** by Ben Wagin features original

Wall segments, each painted with a year and the number of people killed at the border in that year. If the door's not open, sneak a peek through the window.

7 Parlament der Bäume

Wagin also masterminded the **Parliament of Trees**, a memorial consisting of trees, memorial stones, pictures, text, an original section of the barrier and the names of 258 victims inscribed on slabs of granite.

Best Walks
Traipsing Through Tiergarten

🏃 The Walk

Berlin's rulers used to hunt boar and pheasants in the rambling forest-like Tiergarten until Peter Lenné landscaped the grounds in the 18th century. Today, it's one of the world's largest urban parks and a popular place for strolling, jogging, picnicking and, yes, nude tanning. It's also the setting for a huge New Year's Eve party and mega-festivals like the Christopher Street Day parade.

Start Brandenburg Gate; U-/S-Bahn Brandenburger Tor

Finish Potsdamer Platz; U-/S-Bahn Potsdamer Platz

Length 4km; one to 1½ hours

✕ Take a Break

At **Cafe am Neuen See** (Lichtensteinallee 2; ⏱ from 10am daily Mar-Oct, Sat & Sun only Nov-Feb), a lakeside beer garden, cold beers go well with Bratwurst, pretzels and pizza. Romantics can rent a boat and take their sweetie for a spin.

CHRISTOPH BECKER/IMAGEBROKER ©

❶ Strasse des 17 Juni

The broad boulevard bisecting Tiergarten was named **Street of 17 June** in honour of the victims of the bloodily quashed 1953 workers' uprising in East Berlin. Dating back to the 16th century, it originally linked two royal palaces and was doubled in width and turned into a swastika-lined triumphal road under Hitler.

❷ Sowjetisches Ehrenmal

Near the Brandenburg Gate end of the park, the **Soviet War Memorial** is flanked by two Russian T-34 tanks said to have been the first to enter the city in 1945. It was built by German workers on order of the Soviets and completed just months after the end of the war. More than 2000 Red Army soldiers are buried behind the colonnade.

❸ Schloss Bellevue

A succession of German presidents has made their home in snowy-white **Bellevue Palace**.

The neoclassical pile was originally a pad for the youngest brother of King Frederick the Great, then became a school under Kaiser Wilhelm II and a museum of ethnology under the Nazis. It's closed to the public.

❹ Siegessäule

Engulfed by roundabout traffic, the 1873 **Victory Column** was erected to celebrate Prussian military victories and is now a prominent symbol of Berlin's gay community. What would Bismarck think

of that? The gilded lady on top represents the goddess of victory and is featured prominently in the Wim Wenders movie *Wings of Desire*. Climb to the top to appreciate the park's dimensions.

❺ Rousseauinsel

One of Tiergarten's most idyllic spots is the **Rousseauinsel**, a teensy island in a placid pond that's a memorial to 18th-century French philosopher Jean-Jacques Rousseau. It was designed to resemble his actual

burial site on an island near Paris. Just look for the stone pillar.

❻ Luiseninsel

Another enchanting place, **Luiseninsel** is a tranquil gated garden brimming with statues and redolent with seasonal flower beds. It was created after Napoleon's occupying troops left town in 1808 in celebration of the return from exile of the royal couple Friedrich Wilhelm III and Queen Luise.

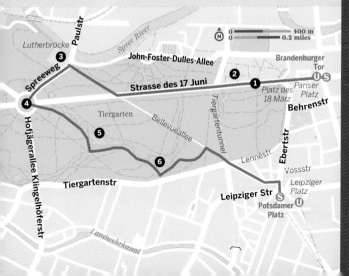

Best
Eating

If you crave traditional comfort food, you'll certainly find plenty of places in Berlin to indulge in roast pork knuckles, smoked pork chops or calves liver. These days, though, 'typical' local fare is lighter, healthier, creative and more likely to come from gourmet kitchens, organic eateries and a UN worth of ethnic restaurants.

Modern German

A growing league of chefs has jumped on the loca-vore bandwagon, letting local, farm-fresh and often organic ingredients steer seasonally calibrated menus. The Michelin testers have confirmed that Berlin is ripe for the culinary big time by awarding their coveted stars to 13 chefs.

Fast-Food Faves

The humble Currywurst, a slivered, subtly spiced pork sausage swimming in tomato sauce and dusted with curry powder, is as iconic as the Brandenburg Gate. The doner kebab is a legacy of Berlin's vast Turkish community.

Ethnic Delights

Berlin's multicultural tapestry has brought the world's foods to town, from Austrian schnitzel to Zambian zebra steaks. Sushi is hugely popular and Mexican and Korean restaurants have been pro-liferating. Reflecting the trend towards tasty and healthy food is the abundance of Asian eateries, especially Thai and Vietnamese.

New Trends

Vegan restaurants have been sprouting quicker than alfalfa, as have 'bio' cafes where dishes are prepared from organic, locally sourced ingredients.

☑ Top Tips

▶ Where phone numbers are listed in this book we recom-mend calling ahead for reservations.

▶ Many restaurants offer value-priced two- or three-course 'business' lunches.

Best Old Berlin

Max und Moritz Meat lovers will be in pig heaven at this century-old gastropub. (pictured above; p94)

Zur Letzten Instanz Industrial-weight speci-alities served with a side of misty-eyed nostalgia since 1621. (p52)

Schusterjunge Cosy corner pub kicks German comfort food into high gear. (p118)

Curry 36

Best Local Eateries

Cafe Jacques First-class culinary journey at economy prices. (p99)

Frau Mittenmang Sassy German dishes paired with house brew and top wines. (p116)

Oderquelle Perfect port of call for oldies but goodies. (p117)

Schwarzer Hahn Slow-food bistro. (p106)

Best Ethnic Eats

Chén Chè Secluded Vietnamese teahouse serves palate-popping plates. (p80)

Uma Tummy-tantalising sushi, grills and Japanese classics. (p35)

Defne Proof there's more to Turkish food than doner kebab. (p92)

Hartweizen A jumping Italian where dishes burst with the feisty flavours of Puglia. (p80)

Best Fine Dining

Borchardt Top Wiener schnitzel in town, with a Rolls-Royce crowd to go with it. (p36)

Fischers Fritz Formal Michelin-starred emporium serves dazzling compositions. (p35)

Horváth Superbly clever but refreshingly down-to-earth despite stratospheric rise to Michelin stardom. (p92)

Best Quick Eats

Burgermeister Ghetto-gourmet burgers served in a former toilet. Really. (p94)

Curry 36 An ode to the Currywurst with a cult crowd following. (p71)

W – der Imbiss Birthplace of 'naan pizza'. (p118)

Dolores Build-your-own burritos and homemade lemonades. (p81)

Best Vegan & Vegetarian

Cookies Cream Cool but comfortable hidden herbivore haven. (p36)

Kopps German comfort food, completely animal-free. (p81)

Best
Bars

Snug pubs, riverside beach bars, beer gardens, spit-and-sawdust dives, DJ bars, snazzy hotel lounges, cocktail caverns – finding a party pen to match your mood is no tall order. Kreuzberg and Friedrichshain have the edgier venues, while Mitte teems with swish drinking dens guarded by doormen. Bars out west are more suited for date night than dedicated drink-a-thons.

Etiquette

Table service is common in German bars and pubs; you shouldn't order at the bar unless you intend to hang out there or there's a sign saying *Selbstbedienung* (self-service). It's customary to have a tab instead of paying for each round separately. Note that in bars with live DJs, €1 is usually added to the cost of your first drink. Drinking in public is legal and widely practised, but be civilised about it. No puking on the U-Bahn, please!

Libations

Predictably, beer is big in Berlin and most places pour a variety of local, national and import brews. *Pils* is the most common draught beer, but bottled *Weizenbier* (wheat beer) also has many takers. The quality of wine ranges from dazzling to abysmal, which is probably why so many Germans drink lesser ones as a spritz, called a *Weinschorle*. German *Sekt* or Italian Prosecco (sparkling wines) have their fans and are often served on the rocks, sometimes with a splash of Aperol. Caipirinhas and mojitos are summertime standbys, but for more complicated concoctions, search out a dedicated cocktail bar. Non-boozers often find *Saftschorle* (fizzy water and juice) a refreshing alternative to the usual carbonated sodas.

☑ Top Tips

▶ The line between cafe and bar is often blurred, with many places changing stripes as the hands move around the clock.

▶ Alcohol is served pretty much all day, and many bars keep pouring until the last tippler leaves.

Best Cocktail Bars

Bebel Bar 'Million Dollar' cocktails in a former bank building. (p37)

Becketts Kopf Where premium mixologists create sublime custom concoctions. (p119)

Würgeengel Bask in the 1960s vintage vibe of this bustling cocktail salon. (pictured above; p89)

Solar

Best Trendy Bars

Trust Trust funds are helpful in this living room of the creative glamour crowd. (p83)

Neue Odessa Bar Comfy thirst parlour teeming with hotties and hopefuls. (p83)

KingSize Bar Good things come in small packages at this well-stocked hole-in-the-wall. (p83)

Tausend Retro-futuristic glamour joint behind unmarked door. (p37)

Best Outdoor Bars

Strandgut Berlin Wiggle your toes in the sand of this chic riverside beach bar. (p108)

Strandbar Mitte Berlin's original beach bar with views of Museum Island. (p53)

Freischwimmer Canalside setting favoured by chillers and party people. (p96)

Club der Visionäre Boatshed turned party pen with DJs that know the groove. (p94)

Best Bars with a View

Solar Stylish and romantic with mellow sounds. (p66)

Puro Sky Lounge Lofty lounge draws wannabe A-listers with money to burn. (p130)

Weekend Take in the lights of Alexanderplatz from the summertime roof terrace. (p53)

Deck 5 Count the steeples from this bar atop a shopping mall. (p119)

Best Beer Gardens

Cafe am Neuen See Beer and pretzels in Tiergarten park. (p148)

Prater Berlin's oldest beer garden. (p118)

Golgatha Alfresco hangout on the Kreuzberg, Berlin's highest natural hill. (p71)

Best DJ Bars

Monarch Bar Beloved gimmick-free Kreuzberg classic. (p88)

Madame Claude Topsy-turvy watering hole. (p96)

Süss War Gestern Loll on sofas in this flirty drinking den. (p108)

Best
Clubs

Berlin is Germany's club capital, the city where techno came of age, the living heart of the European electronic scene and the spiritual home of the lost weekend. Minimal techno, high-speed drum and bass, kick-ass punk, fist-pumping hip hop, beat-free ambient or even swing and tango, there's a place to party any night of the week.

Spinmeisters

With so many top electro DJs living in Berlin – and others happy to visit – the city is a virtual musical testing lab. Line-ups are often amazing. DJ royalty to watch out for includes André Galluzzi, Ellen Allien, Kiki, Sasha Funke, Ricardo Villalobos, Paul Kalkbrenner, Modeselektor, Apparat, M.A.N.D.Y, Tiefschwarz, Gudrun Gut, Booka Shade, Richie Hawtin and too many more to mention.

When to Go

Berlin's notoriously late nights have gotten even later of late. Most clubs and parties don't kick into high gear until about 2am and some go nonstop from Friday night to Monday morning. Some folks put in a good night's sleep, then hit the dance floor when other people head for Sunday church.

At the Door

Top clubs charge €12 or €15 for admission, but elsewhere €3 to €10 is typical. Doors can be tough on busy nights at top clubs like Berghain/Panorama Bar (p108), Watergate (p94) and Cookies (p37), but overall making it past the bouncer is still relatively relaxed. Individual style generally beats high heels and Armani, and if your attitude is right, age rarely matters. If you have to queue, be respectful and don't talk too loudly. Don't arrive wasted.

☑ **Top Tips**

▶ Check **Resident Advisor** (RA; www .residentadvisor.net) for the latest party line-up.

▶ To determine which club best matches your style, go to www.club matcher.de.

▶ Scan RA, flyers, posters and local listings magazines for new openings, one-off raves, festivals, label releases and other parties.

Felix

Best Electro

Berghain Big bad Berghain is still Berlin's quintessential dancing den of iniquity. (p108)

Watergate Two floors, a stunning riverside setting and plenty of eye candy. (p94)

://about blank Wild, trashy, unpredictable and with great garden for daytime chilling. (p108)

K-TV The exterior screams 'dive' but once inside you'll know why it's perennially packed. (p83)

Cookies Sleek and sexy amid GDR-era glamour. (pictured left; p37)

Weekend Lofty lair has the best views and a fabulous rooftop terrace. (p53)

Best Non-Electro

Clärchens Ballhaus Salsa, tango, ballroom, disco and swing's the thing in this grand retro ballroom. (p82)

Kaffee Burger Home of the Russian disco and endless nights of delicious debauchery. (p83)

Felix Well-heeled weekend warriors press the flesh at this tricked-out party pen. (p37)

Worth a Trip

Successor to the legendary Bar 25, **Kater Holzig** (www .katerholzig.de, in German; Michaelkirchstrasse 23; U-Bahn Heinrich-Heine-Strasse) is a wickedly raving riverside playground set around a graffiti-doused old soap factory. The door is as tough as ever, but beyond it awaits a dark techno floor, a cosy saloon with stage for live bands, plus the Katerschmaus restaurant decked out in trippy graffiti-glam decor.

Best
Live Music

There's no need to go a day without music in Berlin. With at least 2000 active bands, lots of venues large and small, and dozens of indie labels, the city is Germany's undisputed capital of sound. Berliners are also enthusiastic supporters of jazz and classical music with no fewer than seven state-supported orchestras, including the world-famous Berliner Symphoniker.

Best Rock, Pop & Indie

Magnet Good chance to see tomorrow's headliners today. (p96)

Lido Plenty of big names in fairly intimate setting, plus rocking club nights. (p96)

Astra Kulturhaus Head-bobbing platform for indie bands, big names included. (p109)

Best Jazz & Blues

B-Flat Programming that mixes no-namers with big-timers for a serious and respectful audience. (pictured above; p84)

Yorckschlösschen No-nonsense pub-like venue for low-key cool cats. (p71)

A-Trane Intimate been-there-forever saloon known for attracting major talent and legendary jam sessions. (p131)

Best Classical

Berliner Philharmonie One of the world's best orchestras within its own 'cathedral of sound'. (p67)

Konzerthaus Berlin Schinkel-built jewel on Gendarmenmarkt. (p38)

Worth a Trip

Waldbühne (www.wald buehne-berlin.de; Am Glock-enturm; S-Bahn Pichelsberg) Summers in Berlin just wouldn't be the same without this chill spot for symphonies under the stars, big-name rock, jazz and comedy acts and film presentations. The

1936 open-air amphitheatre in the woods is about 8km west of Zoologischer Garten, next to the Olympic Stadium.

Best
Cabaret &
Performance

Berliners are enthusiastic supporters of the arts and venues are often filled to capacity. Not many cities afford themselves the luxury of three state-funded opera houses and theatre too has a long tradition, as do Golden Twenties–style variety shows. Light, lively and lavish, these have been undergoing a sweeping revival and are often held in glamorous venues.

ALAMY/CELEBRITY / ALAMY ©

Best Theatre

Berliner Ensemble
Bertolt Brecht's old theatre is still going strong with newly inter-preted German classics. (p38)

Admiralspalast Recently revived 1920s perform-ance palace presents eclectic programming from dance to theatre to comedy. (pictured above; p38)

Best Cabaret

Chamäleon Varieté
Intimate former ballroom delivers an alchemy of acrobatics, artistry and sex appeal. (p84)

Bar Jeder Vernunft
Gorgeous mirrored tent makes you feel as if you're on the set of *Cabaret*. (p130)

Friedrichstadtpalast
Europe's largest revue theatre puts on sparkly Vegas-style shows. (p84)

Worth a Trip

Staatsoper (www .staatsoper-berlin.de; Bismarckstrasse 110; U-Bahn Ernst-Reuter-Platz) Point your highbrow compass towards the Daniel Barenboim–led Staatsoper, Berlin's top opera company. While its historic digs on Unter den Linden are under renovation, high-calibre productions are staged at the Schiller Theater.

☑ **Top Tips**

▶ Many theatres are closed on Mondays and in July and August.

Deutsche Oper Berlin
(www.deutscheoperberlin .de; Bismarckstrasse 35; U-Bahn Deutsche Oper) The city's other opera house is just down the street. All operas are sung in their original language.

Best
Gay & Lesbian

Berlin's legendary liberalism has spawned one of the world's biggest, most divine and diverse GLBT playgrounds. Anything goes in 'Homopolis' (and we *do* mean anything!), from the highbrow to the hands-on, the bourgeois to the bizarre, the mainstream to the flamboyant. Except for the most hardcore places, gay spots get their share of opposite-sex and straight patrons.

Gay Areas

The closest that Berlin has to a 'gay village' is Schöneberg (Motzstrasse and Fuggerstrasse especially), where the rainbow flag has proudly flown since the 1920s. There's plenty of partying but it's pretty old-school and anyone under 35 will likely feel more comfortable elsewhere. Current hipster central is Kreuzberg, which teems with party pens, especially along Oranienstrasse and Mehringdamm. Across the river, Friedrichshain has fewer gay bars but such key clubs as Berghain/Panorama Bar and the hardcore Lab.oratory. In Prenzlauer Berg gay-geared locales are fairly spread out.

Party Spectrum

Berlin's gayscape ranges from mellow cafes, campy bars and cinemas to saunas, cruising areas, clubs with darkrooms and all-out sex venues. In fact, sex and sexuality are entirely everyday matters to the unshockable city folk and there are very few, if any, itches that can't be quite openly and legally scratched. As elsewhere, gay men have more options, but grrrrls – from lipstick lesbians to bad-ass dykes – need not feel left out either.

Some of the best club nights are independent of venues and may move around. Check the websites or magazines for the latest scoop.

☑ Top Tips

▶ The weekly freebie magazine **Siegessäule** (www.siegessaeule.de, in German) is the Berlin bible for all things gay and lesbian.

▶ The free English/German booklet **Out in Berlin** (www.out-in-berlin.de) is another indispensable guide.

▶ The gay online dating site of choice in Berlin is www.gayromeo.com.

Christopher Street Day Parade (Berlin's Pride march)

Best Bars & Cafes

Roses Plush, pink, tacky, campy madhouse is an essential experience. (p89)

Cafe Berio Retro-styled coffeehouse sports motto 'enjoy, relax, flirt'. Words to live by. (p133)

Möbel Olfe Usually mixed but gays rule on Thursdays. (p89)

Zum Schmutzigen Hobby Trash diva Nina Queer's louche lair is not for the faint-of-heart. (p108)

Himmelreich Low-key, comfortable and conversationalist with great cakes on weekends. (p109)

Marietta On Wednesdays, this retro bar is a warm-up for the local gay party circuit. (p119)

Best Clubs & Parties

Berghain Post-industrial techno-electro hellhole for studly queer bass junkies; with darkrooms. (p108)

Weekend Host of GMF, Berlin's premier Sunday club, known for excessive SM (standing and modelling). (p53)

Bassy Trash diva Chantal's 'House of Shame' parties on Thursday run wild and wicked. (p119)

SO36 Gay parties include the rainbow tea dance Cafe Fatal on Sunday nights. (p89)

Worth a Trip

SchwuZ (www .schwuz.de, in German; Mehringdamm 61; ⏱ Wed, Fri & Sat; U-Bahn Mehringdamm) in western Kreuzberg is a queer institution and a friendly place to ease into the scene. Fortify yourself at the street-front cafe-bar **Melitta Sundström**, then drop down to the cellar to flirt with locals over a high-energy mix of retro hits, glam pop and alt-rock. Lesbians take over during **L-Tunes** on the last Saturday of the month.

Best
Art

Home to more than 10,000 artists, bristling with imagination and optimism, Berlin has become a cauldron of cultural cool. It has more galleries than New York City (around 600) alongside an impressive roster of museums showcasing a who's who of creative hotshots over the past 1500 years.

Getting Visual

Art aficionados will find their compass on perpetual spin in Berlin, which has developed the most exciting and dynamic arts scene in Europe. There have been some notable breakthroughs, most famously by Danish-Icelandic artist Olafur Eliasson. Other major contemporary artists living and working in Berlin include Thomas Demand, Jonathan Meese, Via Lewandowsky, Isa Genzken, Tino Seghal, Esra Ersen, John Bock and the artist duo Ingar Dragset und Michael Elmgreen.

Gallery Quarters

Established galleries are prevalent in the Scheunenviertel, especially along Linienstrasse and Auguststrasse, and along Kurfürstendamm's side streets such as Fasanenstrasse. The Checkpoint Charlie area mixes old hands on Zimmerstrasse and newcomers, mostly on Markgrafenstrasse. Over the past couple of years, Potsdamer Strasse south of Potsdamer Platz has also emerged as a hotspot, with some major galleries decamping to this gritty part of Schöneberg.

☑ Top Tips

▶ The Berlin Museum Pass (€19) buys entry to about 70 museums for three consecutive days. Available at participating museums.

▶ **GoArt** (www.goart -berlin.de) demystifies Berlin's art scene on customised tours by visiting private collections, artist studios and exciting galleries and street art locations.

Best Art Events

Berlin Biennale (www .berlinbiennale.de) Explore international trends.

Gallery Weekend (www .gallery-weekend-berlin.de) A free hop around the city's best galleries.

Alte Nationalgalerie

Best Art Museums

Gemäldegalerie An astounding Aladdin's cave of Old Masters. (p56)

Neue Nationalgalerie 20th-century hotshots on parade in an edgy glass house. (pictured left; p64)

Alte Nationalgalerie World's finest Romanticists and Realists. (p50)

Best Contemporary Galleries

KW Institute for Contemporary Art Tomorrow's art-world heavyweights. (p79)

Sammlung Boros World-class contemporaries. (p79)

DaimlerContemporary International abstract, conceptual and minimalist art. (p61)

Deutsche Guggenheim Berlin Happy blend of art and money showcases new work by contemporary greats. (p35)

Best Niche Collections

Museum Berggruen Priceless Picassos, plus works by Klee and Giacometti. (p136)

Sammlung Scharf-Gerstenberg Enter the surreal fantasy worlds of such artists as Goya and Dalí. (p136)

Käthe-Kollwitz-Museum A paean to the greatest German 20th-century woman artist. (p126)

Emile Nolde Museum Brightly pigmented landscapes and nature scenes by leading German expressionist. (p33)

Worth a Trip

Berlin's premier contemporary art museum, **Hamburger Bahnhof** (www.hamburgerbahn hof.de; Invalidenstrasse 50-51; adult/concession €8/4; ⏱10am-6pm Tue-Fri, 11am-8pm Sat, 11am-6pm Sun; U-/S-Bahn Hauptbahnhof) presents works by Andy Warhol, Roy Lichtenstein, Anselm Kiefer and other heavyweights in a cleverly converted 19th-century railway station and 300m-long warehouse. It's just a five-minute walk east of the Hauptbahnhof.

Best
Architecture

After visiting the German capital in 1891, Mark Twain remarked, 'Berlin is the newest city I've ever seen.' True then, still true now. Destruction and division have ensured that today's city is essentially a creation of modern times, a showcase of 20th-century styles with only a sprinkling of vestiges surviving from earlier times.

Post-Reunification

Reunification presented Berlin with both the challenge and the opportunity to redefine itself architecturally. With the Wall gone, huge gashes of empty space opened up where the city halves were to be rejoined. The grandest of the post-1990 developments is Potsdamer Platz, a contemporary interpretation of the famous historic square. More cutting-edge architecture awaits in the government quarter, especially with the Bundeskanzleramt (p25) and the updated historic Reichstag (p25).

The Schinkel Touch

It was Karl Friedrich Schinkel (1781–1841) who stamped his imprimatur on the face of Prussian Berlin. The most prominent architect of German neoclassicism, his buildings strove for the perfect balance between functionality and beauty, achieved through clear lines, symmetry and an impeccable sense for aesthetics.

The 1920s & the Bauhaus

The spirit of innovation brought some of the finest avant-garde architects to Berlin in the 1920s, including Le Corbusier, Ludwig Mies van der Rohe and Hans Scharoun. Their association later evolved into the Bauhaus, which used practical anti-elitist principles to unite form and function and had a profound effect on modern aesthetics.

Best of Schinkel

Altes Museum Grand colonnaded front inspired by a philosopher's school in Athens. (p49)

Konzerthaus Berlin Sweeping staircase leads to a raised columned portico of this famous concert hall. (p38)

Neue Wache Royal guardhouse blends Roman fort outline with Greek temple facade. (p33)

Best Prussian

Brandenburg Gate This triumphal arch is Germany's best-known landmark. (p26)

Schloss Charlottenburg Pretty Prussian power display. (p134)

Schloss Sanssouci Frederick the Great's rococo retreat. (p138)

Architect Hans Scharoun's Berliner Philharmonie

Berliner Dom Former royal court church in exuberant Italian Renaissance style. (p50)

Best Post-WWII

Neue Nationalgalerie Glass-and-steel stunner by Ludwig Mies van der Rohe. (p64)

Berliner Philharmonie Eccentric concert hall is Hans Scharoun's modernist masterpiece. (p67)

Haus der Kulturen der Welt Avant-garde structure with gravity-defying sculptural roof. (p38)

Best Post-1989

Jüdisches Museum Daniel Libeskind's zigzag-shaped architectural metaphor for Jewish history. (p68)

Neues Museum David Chipperfield's reconstructed New Museum ingeniously blends old and new. (p46)

Sony Center Helmut Jahn's svelte glass-and-steel complex is the most striking on Potsdamer Platz. (pictured left; p61)

IM Pei Bau Strikingly geometrical, glass-spiral-fronted museum annexe by the 'Mandarin of Modernism'. (p32)

Worth a Trip

Built by the Nazis for the 1936 Olympic Games, the **Olympic Stadium** (☎ 2500 2322; www.olympiastadion -berlin.de; Olympischer Platz 3; self-guided tour adult/concession €4/3; ◷ daily; S-Bahn Olympiastadion) was completely modernised for the 2006 FIFA World Cup when its bombastic bulk was softened by the addition of a spidery oval roof. It hosts soccer games, concerts and mega-events and can be toured on non-event days.

Best
Historical Sites

In Berlin the past is always present. Strolling around boulevards and neighbourhoods, you can't help but pass by legendary sights that take you back to the era of Prussian glory, the dark ages of the Third Reich, the tense period of the Cold War and the euphoria of reunification. Like a 3D textbook, only better.

The Age of Prussia

Berlin has been a royal residence ever since Elector Friedrich III was elevated to King Friedrich I in 1701. This promotion significantly shaped the city, which blossomed under Frederick the Great, who sought greatness as much on the battlefield as through building. In the 19th century, Prussia weathered revolutions and industrialisation to forge the creation of the German Reich, which lasted until the monarchy's demise in 1918.

Berlin under the Nazi Nadir

No other political power shaped the 20th century as much as Nazi Germany. The megalomania of Hitler and his henchmen wrought destruction upon much of Europe, bringing death to at least 50 million people, and forever realigned the world order. Few original sites remain, but memorials and museums keep the horror a focus.

Cold War Chills

After WWII, Germany fell into the crosshairs of the Cold War, a country divided along ideological lines by the victorious powers, its internal border marked by fences and a wall. Just how differently the two countries developed is still very palpable in Berlin, expressed not only through Berlin Wall remnants such as the East Side Gallery but also through vastly different urban planning and architectural styles.

Best of Prussian Glory

Brandenburg Gate
Royal city gate is Germany's most iconic national symbol. (p26)

Reichstag Stand in awe of history at the palatial home of the German parliament. (p24)

Schloss Charlottenburg Palace provides a glimpse into the lifestyles of the rich and royal. (p134)

Siegessäule A giant gilded goddess crowns the top of the soaring Victory Column. (pictured above; p149)

Holocaust Memorial

Best of Third Reich

Holocaust Memorial
Commemorates the unspeakable horrors of the WWII Jewish genocide. (p28)

Topographie des Terrors Peels away the many layers of brutality of the Nazi state. (p63)

Gedenkstätte Deutscher Widerstand Commemorates the brave men and women of the German Nazi resistance. (p64)

Best of Red Berlin

East Side Gallery The longest remaining stretch of the Berlin Wall turned art canvas. (p102)

Gedenkstätte Berliner Mauer Germany's central memorial to the victims of the Berlin Wall. (p74)

Karl-Marx-Allee East Berlin's pompous yet impressive main boulevard and showpiece of socialist architecture. (p106)

Tränenpalast Learn about the personal toll Germany's division took on ordinary citizens. (p32)

Checkpoint Charlie The famous border crossing was a Cold War hotspot. (p63)

Worth a Trip

Victims of persecution by the GDR-era Ministry for State Security (Stasi) often ended up in the grim **Stasi Prison** (www.stiftung-hsh.de; Genslerstrasse 13a; adult/concession €5/2.50; English tours 2.30pm Wed & Sat, German tours daily; M5 to Freienwalder Strasse). Tours reveal the full extent of the terror and cruelty perpetrated by this sinister institution upon thousands of suspected regime opponents, many of them utterly innocent.

Best
Museums

Best History Museums

Deutsches Historisches Museum Comprehensive journey through 2000 years of Germany's turbulent past. (pictured right; p32)

Story of Berlin Berlin history bundled in a neat, edutaining multimedia package. (p127)

Jüdisches Museum Goes beyond the Holocaust in tracing the history of Jews in Germany. (p68)

DDR Museum Engaging look at daily life behind the Iron Curtain. (p49)

Best Niche Museums

Bröhan Museum Beautiful objects and furniture from the art deco, art nouveau and functionalist periods. (p136)

Museum The Kennedys Tribute to the ill-fated American president and his family. (p27)

Museum für Naturkunde Meet giant dinos in Berlin's own 'Jurassic Park'. (p79)

Museum für Film und Fernsehen An entertaining romp through German celluloid history. (p61)

Museum für Fotografie Spotlight on the oeuvre of fashion and lifestyle photographer Helmut Newton. (p126)

Best Antiquities

Pergamonmuseum Treasure trove of monumental architecture from ancient civilisations. (p42)

Altes Museum Gorgeous Schinkel building sheltering priceless Greek, Etruscan and Roman art and sculpture. (p49)

Neues Museum Pay your respects to Egyptian Queen Nefertiti and her entourage. (p46)

Worth a Trip

Stasi Museum (www .stasimuseum.de; House 1, Ruschestrasse 103; adult/concession €5/4; ⏰11am-6pm Mon-Fri, 2-6pm Sat & Sun; U-Bahn Magdalenenstrasse) The former

☑ **Top Tips**

▶ For many museums you can buy tickets in advance online, allowing you to skip the queues.

▶ Museum lovers should invest in the Berlin Museum Pass (€19; available at participating museums), which gives entry to about 70 museums for a three-day period.

head office of the GDR's Ministry for State Security (Stasi) is now a museum, where you can see a prisoner transport van, cunningly low-tech surveillance devices (hidden in watering cans, rocks, even neckties) and the obsessively neat offices of Stasi chief Erich Mielke.

Best
Quiet Spots

If your head is spinning with all the stimulus Berlin is throwing at you, there are plenty of places that can provide a restorative antidote. Funtastic outdoor spots and serene retreats lurk in every neighbourhood.

RICHARD NEBESKY/LONELY PLANET IMAGES ©

Best Parks & Gardens

Tiergarten Get lost amid the lawns, trees and paths of this enormous city park. (p148)

Schlossgarten Charlottenburg Set up a picnic near the carp pond and ponder royal splendours. (pictured right; p135)

Park Sanssouci Find your favourite spot away from the crowds in this sprawling royal park. (p138)

Best Cemeteries

Alter Jüdischer Friedhof Berlin's oldest Jewish cemetery was destroyed by the Nazis. (p80)

Jüdischer Friedhof Schönhauser Allee Final resting place of the painter Max Liebermann and other prominent Berlin Jews. (p116)

Best Memorial Sites

Neue Wache An anti-war memorial centred on an emotional Käthe Kollwitz sculpture. (p33)

Holocaust Memorial An outsized maze of stelae represents this outsized crime against humanity. (p28)

Luftbrückendenkmal Pay tribute to a true 'triumph of the will' at the Berlin Airlift memorial. (p71)

Best Churches

Berliner Dom Royal court church cuts a commanding presence on Museum Island. (p50)

Gethsemanekirche Beautiful 19th-century church played key role in collapse of the GDR. (p116)

Worth a Trip

Soviet War Memorial (admission free; ☉24hr; S-Bahn Treptower Park) South of Kreuzberg, at the heart of Treptower Park, this gargantuan memorial shelters the graves of 5000 Soviet soldiers killed in the Battle of Berlin, a sobering testament to the immensity of the country's wartime losses. It's past the stone gate, about 750m southeast of the S-Bahn station via Puschkinallee.

Best
Shopping

Berlin is a great place to shop, and we're definitely not talking malls and chains. The city's appetite for the individual manifests itself in small, unique boutiques that are a pleasure to explore. Shopping here is as much about visual stimulus as it is about actual purchasing power. Whether you're frugal or a power-shopper, you'll find plenty of intriguing purchases.

Where to Shop

The closest Berlin comes to having a shopping boulevard is Kurfürstendamm (Ku'damm) and its extension, Tauentzienstrasse. They're largely the purview of the mainstream retailers you probably know from back home, from Mango to H&M to Levi's and Esprit. You'll find more of the same in malls such as Alexa and Potsdamer Platz Arkaden.

Getting the most out of shopping in Berlin means venturing off the high street and into the *Kieze* (neighbourhoods). This is where you'll discover a cosmopolitan cocktail of indie boutiques stirred by the city's zest for life and entrepreneurial spirit. Each *Kiez* comes with its own flair, identity and mix of stores calibrated to the needs, tastes and bank accounts of local residents.

Opening Hours

Department stores, supermarkets and shops in major commercial districts (such as Kurfürstendamm) and malls usually open at 10am and close at 8pm or later. Boutiques and other smaller shops keep flexible hours, opening sometime mid-morning and generally closing at 7pm, sometimes earlier on Saturday. Stores are closed on Sunday, except for some bakeries, supermarkets, flower shops and souvenir shops. Also see p178.

☑ Top Tips

▶ Most stores, especially smaller ones, do not accept credit cards.

▶ To get your fix on a Sunday, head to Berlin's fabulous flea markets.

Best Bookstores

Dussmann – Das Kulturkaufhaus The mother lode of books and music with late opening hours. (p39)

Best Flea Markets

Mauerpark Crowded as hell but still urban archaeology at its finest and funnest. (p113)

Arkonaplatz Smaller and less frantic, this is an essential stop for retro fans. (p120)

Galeries Lafayette

Boxhagener Platz
Treasure-hunting
grounds with plenty of
entertainment, cafes and
people-watching. (p109)

Best Made in Berlin

Ausberlin Great for
scene-savvy label
hunters. (p53)

Bonbonmacherei Find a
new favourite in this old-
fashioned candy kitchen.
(p84)

Frau Tonis Parfum Get a
customised scent. (p67)

Ta(u)sche Ingenious
messenger bags with
changeable flaps to lug
your Berlin purchases.
(p121)

Ampelmann Galerie
Berlin's iconic traffic-light
man on T-shirts, towels
and more. (p85)

Best Food & Drink

KaDeWe Luxe depart-
ment store's 6th floor is
foodie heaven with mas-
sive selections of first-
rate anything. (p131)

Fassbender & Rausch
The finest pralines and
truffles, plus Berlin landmarks built of chocolate.
(pictured left; p39)

1. Absinth Depot Berlin
Make a date with the
'green fairy' at this ec-
centric depot. (p85)

Best Malls & Department Stores

Galeries Lafayette
Brings buckets of French
je ne sais quoi to the
German capital. (p39)

KaDeWe Lug time and
platinum cards to do jus-
tice to Berlin's equivalent
of Harrods. (p131)

Friedrichstadtpassagen
Trio of posh arcades
where designer stores
compete with the gor-
geous interior design.
(p39)

Best Quirky Stores

Erfinderladen Berlin
Source unique inven-
tions you never knew you
could live without. (p120)

Luxus International
One-of-a-kind souvenirs
made by emerging
creatives. (p121)

Killerbeast Perfect for
true individualists, this
store makes new cloth-
ing from secondhand
garments. (p97)

Mondos Arts Cult
classics from the GDR –
hen-shaped egg cups to
condoms. (p109)

Best
Tours

If you're a Berlin first-timer, letting someone else show you around is a great way to get your bearings, see the key sights quickly and obtain a general understanding of the city. All manner of exploration – from generic city bus tours to special-interest outings – are available.

Walking & Cycling Tours

Several companies offer both English-language general city explorations and themed tours (eg Third Reich, Cold War, Potsdam) that don't require reservations – you just show up at the designated meeting point. Since these change quite frequently, look for flyers in hotel or hostel lobbies or check online. Some guides work for tips only but the better tours cost between €10 and €15.

Boat Tours

A lovely way to experience Berlin on a warm day is from the deck of a boat cruising the city's rivers, canals and lakes. Tours range from one-hour spins around the historic centre (from €9) to longer trips to Schloss Charlottenburg and beyond (from €13.50). Most offer live narration in English and German and sell refreshments on board. Embarkation points are concentrated near Museum Island.

Bus Tours

You'll see them everywhere around town: colourful buses (in summer, often open-top double-deckers) that tick off all the key sights on two-hour loops with basic taped commentary in multiple languages. You're free to get off and back on at any of the stops. Buses depart roughly every 15 or 30 minutes between 10am and 5pm or 6pm daily; tickets cost from €10 to €20.

☑ Top Tips

▶ Get a crash course in 'Berlinology' by hopping on the upper deck of public **bus 100 or 200** (€2.30) at Zoologischer Garten or Alexanderplatz and letting the landmarks whoosh by.

▶ For a DIY walk along the path of the Berlin Wall, rent a multimedia **Mauerguide** (WallGuide; www.mauerguide.com; per day €10). Available at Checkpoint Charlie, the Berlin Wall Memorial and inside the Brandenburger Tor U-Bahn station.

Brandenburg Gate

Best Walking & Cycling Tours

Berlin Walks (☎301 9194; www.berlinwalks.de) Get under the city's historical skin with the local expert guides of Berlin's oldest English-language walking tour company.

Berlin on Bike (☎4373 9999; www.berlinonbike.de) Repertory includes a superb Berlin Wall bike tour and intriguing 'nightseeing' excursions.

Brewer's Berlin Tours (☎0177-388 1537; www.brewersberlintours.com) Purveyors of the epic all-day Best of Berlin tour (foot massage not included) and shorter free tours.

New Berlin Tours (☎5105 0030; www.newberlintours.com)

Energetic and entertaining city spins by the pioneers of the 'free tour' and the pub crawl.

Best Speciality Tours

Berliner Unterwelten (☎4991 0517; www.berliner-unterwelten.de; tours €10-13) Explore Berlin's dark, dank underbelly by picking your way past hospital beds, wartime helmets and filter systems on a tour of WWII-era bunkers, shelters and tunnels.

Fritz Music Tours (☎3087 5633; www.musictours-berlin.com; tours €19) Get the low-down on Berlin's legendary music history – from Bowie to U2, cult clubs to the Love Parade – on this dynamic bus tour. Also: private

minibus tours, walking tours and tours of the Hansa recording studios.

Trabi Safari (☎2759 2273; www.trabi-safari.de; per person €30-60) Catch the *Good Bye, Lenin!* vibe on a tour of Berlin's 'Wild East' from behind the steering wheel of a GDR-era Trabant car (Trabi) with live commentary piped into your vehicle.

Berlinagenten (☎4372 0701; www.berlinagenten .com; 3hr tours for groups up to 6 from €300) Get a handle on the unique Berlin lifestyle with this clued-in company that whisks you behind the scenes of hot bars, boutiques, restaurants and clubs. For an insider's primer on the culinary scene, book a Gastro-Rallye.

Best
With Kids

Travelling to Berlin with kids can be child's play, especially if you keep a light schedule and involve them in the day-to-day planning. There's plenty to do to keep the youngsters occupied, from zoos to kid-oriented museums to magic and puppet shows. Parks and imaginative playgrounds abound in all neighbourhoods, as do public pools.

Legoland Discovery Centre (www.legoland discoverycentre.com; Sony Center, Potsdamer Strasse 4; adult/child €16/13; ◷10am-7pm, last admission 5pm; U-/S-Bahn Potsdamer Platz) Indoor amusement park with 4D cinema, a Lego 'factory', a Jungle Trail where Lego crocs lurk in the dark, a Dragon Castle 'slow-lercoaster' ride and a mini-Berlin with landmarks built entirely from those tiny plastic bricks.

Sea Life Berlin (www .visitsealife.com/berlin; Spandauer Strasse 3; adult/concession €17/12; ◷10am-7pm, last admission 6pm; ⟦100, 200, TXL) This aquarium follows the Spree River into the North Atlantic, introducing you to local aquatic denizens along the way.

Visits conclude with a glacial lift ride through AquaDom (pictured right), a 25m-tall cylindrical tropical fish tank.

Madame Tussauds Berlin (www.madame tussauds.com/berlin; Unter den Linden 74; adult/ concession €20/19; ◷10am-7pm, last admission 6pm; U-/S-Bahn Brandenburger Tor) No celebrity in town to snare your stare? Don't fret: at this legendary wax museum Lady Gaga, Robert Pattinson and Obama stand still – very still – for you to snap their picture.

Deutsches Technikmuseum (German Museum of Technology; www.dtmb.de; Trebbiner Strasse 9; adult/ concession €4.50/2.50; ◷9am-5.30pm Tue-Fri, 10am-6pm Sat & Sun; U-Bahn Möckernbrücke) This giant shrine to

technology counts the world's first computer, an entire hall of vintage locomotives and extensive exhibits on aviation and navigation among its top attractions. At the adjacent **Spectrum science centre** (enter from Möckernstrasse 26; admission included), kids can participate in more than 200 hands-on experiments.

Survival Guide

Survival Guide

Before You Go

When to Go

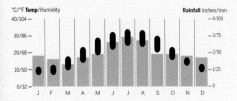

°C/°F **Temp**/Humidity

Rainfall inches/mm

40/104 —   — 4/100

30/86 —   — 3/75

20/68 —   — 2/50

10/50 —   — 1/25

0/32 —   — 0

J F M A M J J A S O N D

➡ **Winter (Nov–Feb)**
Cold and dark, snow possible. Sights are quieter; theatre and concert season is in full swing.

➡ **Spring (Mar–May)**
Mild, often sunny. Sights start getting busy; festival season kicks off; beer gardens and outdoor cafes open.

➡ **Summer (Jun–Aug)**
Warm to hot, often sunny, thunderstorms possible. Peak tourist season; sights and museums are super-busy; life moves outdoors.

➡ **Autumn (Sep–Oct)**
Mild, often sunny. Theatre, concert and football (soccer) seasons start up.

Book Your Stay

☑ **Top Tip** To minimise travel time, avoid staying i a hotel located outside the S-Bahn ring.

➡ With more hotel beds than New York, competition is fierce among Berli properties and prices low compared to other capita cities.

➡ The most central distric is Mitte. Hotels around Kurfürstendamm are plen tiful and close to the trad fairgrounds, but put you a U-Bahn ride away from most blockbuster sights and happening nightlife.

➡ Kreuzberg and Friedric shain are ideal districts if you want to stay within stumbling distance of ba and clubs.

➡ Berlin has a vibrant hostel scene with dorm beds starting at just €9 per night.

➡ Budget designer hotels with chic interiors but minimal amenities are all the rage.

▶ Nostalgic types should check into an old-fashioned B&B, called Hotel-Pension or simply Pension; most prevalent in western districts, especially around Kurfürstendamm.

▶ Furnished flats are a popular alternative to hotels.

▶ Seasonal room-rate variations are rare but prices spike during major trade shows, festivals and public holidays.

▶ Reservations are always a good idea.

▶ Many properties set aside rooms or entire floors for nonsmokers.

Useful Websites

Visit Berlin (www.visitberlin.de) Official tourist office books rooms at partner hotels.

Go Mio (www.gomio.com) Hostel bookings without fee.

HRS (www.hrs.com) General site but especially good for last-minute bargains.

Booking.com (www.booking.com) General site, often has bargains.

Lonely Planet (www.lonelyplanet.com/hotels) Author-penned reviews of Lonely Planet's top choices.

Best Budget

Circus Hostel & Hotel (www.circus-berlin.de) Perennial Scheunenviertel favourite scores high for comfort, cleanliness and thoughtful touches to ease life on the road.

EastSeven Berlin Hostel (www.eastseven.de) Spotless, well run and central with charming staff and chilled ambience in Prenzlauer Berg.

Meininger Hotel & Hostel (www.meininger-hotels.com) Top-flight chain with mod rooms; run with panache and professionalism.

Motel One Berlin-Alexanderplatz (www.motel-one.de) Smallish rooms but up-to-the-minute amenities normally the staple of posher players.

Best Midrange

Hotel Honigmond (www.honigmond-berlin.de) Plenty of historic touches in this elegant Scheunenviertel charmer.

Amano Hotel (www.hotel-amano.com) Super-central budget designer abode in the Scheunenviertel with a great bar.

Michelberger Hotel (www.michelbergerhotel.com) Fun base with eccentric design near East Side Gallery.

Hotel Otto (www.hotelotto.com) Fall-over-backwards staff, fabulous breakfast and free afternoon cake and snacks near Kurfürstendamm.

Best Top End

Hotel de Rome (www.hotelderome.com) Winning alchemy of historic and contemporary in 19th-century bank building on Unter den Linden.

Adlon Kempinski (www.hotel-adlon.de) Berlin's most high-profile defender of the grand tradition, across from Brandenburg Gate.

Mandala Hotel (www.themandala.de) Fashionable, discreet all-suite retreat right on Potsdamer Platz.

Casa Camper (www.casacamper.com) Plenty of design cachet, day-lit bathrooms and lounge with free breakfast and refreshments in Scheunenviertel.

Short-Stay Apartments

Brilliant Apartments (www.brilliant-apartments.de) Seven stylish units with full kitchens in Prenzlauer Berg.

T&C Apartments (www.tc -apartments-berlin.de) Nicely furnished and well-kept apartments and flats in Prenzlauer Berg, Mitte and Schöneberg.

All Berlin Apartments (www.all-berlin-apartments .com) A wide range of good-value, well-appointed apartments in various neighbourhoods.

Be My Guest (www.be-my -guest.com) Good selection of handpicked apart-ments located through-out the city.

Miniloft Berlin (www.miniloft .com) Eight lofts with mod-ern designer furniture and kitchenettes in northern Scheunenviertel.

Arriving in Berlin

☑ **Top Tip** For the best way to get to your accom-modation, see p17.

From Berlin-Tegel Airport

➡ The TXL bus connects Tegel to Alexanderplatz (40 minutes) every 10 minutes. For Kurfürsten-damm and Zoologischer Garten take bus X9 (20 minutes).

➡ You need a transport ticket covering zones AB (€2.30).

➡ The closest U-Bahn station to the airport is Jakob-Kaiser-Platz (served by bus 109 and X9).

➡ Taxis cost about €20 to Zoologischer Garten and €23 to Alexander-platz and take 30 to 45 minutes.

From Berlin-Schönefeld Airport

➡ Airport-Express trains make the 30-minute trip between the airport and central Berlin twice hourly. Note: these are regular regional trains, identified as RE7 and RB14 in timetables.

➡ The S-Bahn S9 runs every 20 minutes and is slower but useful if you're headed to Friedrichshain or Prenzlauer Berg.

➡ Trains stop about 400m from the terminals. Free shuttle buses run every 10 minutes; walking takes about five minutes.

➡ You need a transport ticket covering zones ABC (€3).

➡ Taxi rides average €40 and take 35 minutes to an hour.

From Berlin Brandenburg Airport

➡ Service to Berlin's new airport (under construc-tion next to Schönefeld Airport since 2006) is expected to start on 3 June 2012. When it opens, flights to Tegel and the old Schönefeld airport will reportedly discontinue.

➡ Airport-Express trains depart for central Berlin from the airport's own station every 15 minutes You need a transport ticket covering zones ABC (€3).

➡ For the latest informa-tion, check www.berlin -airport.de.

From Hauptbahnhc

➡ Berlin's central train station is served by buses, the S-Bahn and the U-Bahn.

➡ Taxis wait outside the main (north) entrance. The average fare to Alexanderplatz is about €13, to Zoologischer Garten €12.

Getting Around

U-Bahn

☑ **Best for**... Getting around Berlin quickly.

U-Bahn lines are designated as U1, U2, etc in this book.

Trains operate from 4am until about 12.30am and throughout the night on Friday, Saturday and public holidays (all lines except U4 and U55).

➜ From Sunday through Thursday, night buses (designated N2, N5, etc) follow the U-Bahn routes between 12.30am and 4am at 30-minute intervals.

➜ For information and trip planning, see www .bvg.de.

S-Bahn

☑ **Best for**... Covering longer distances within Berlin.

➜ S-Bahn trains run on the main tracks and make fewer stops than the U-Bahn. Denoted as S1, S2, etc in this book, they operate from 4am to 12.30am and all night on Friday, Saturday and public holidays.

➜ Details are available at www.s-bahn-berlin.de.

Bus

☑ **Best for**... City sightseeing on the cheap.

➜ City buses run frequently between 4.30am and 12.30am.

Tickets & Passes

➜ The public transport network is operated by the BVG. For trip planning and general information, call the 24-hour hotline (☎194 49) or go to www.bvg.de.

➜ One ticket is good on all forms of public transport. Most trips within Berlin require an AB ticket (€2.30), valid for two hours (interruptions and transfers allowed, round trips not). The short-trip ticket (*Kurzstreckenticket*; €1.40) is good for three stops on any U-Bahn or S-Bahn or six on any bus or tram.

➜ Children aged six to 14 qualify for reduced (*ermässigt*) rates, while kids under six travel free.

➜ One-day travel passes (*Tageskarte*) are valid for unlimited travel on all forms of public transport until 3am the following day. The cost for the AB zone is €6.30. Group day passes (*Kleingruppenkarte*) are valid for up to five people travelling together and cost €15.

➜ Buy tickets from vending machines in U- or S-Bahn stations and aboard trams, from bus drivers and at station offices and news kiosks sporting the yellow BVG logo. Don't buy tickets from scammers selling used ones outside stations.

➜ All tickets except those bought from bus drivers must be stamped before boarding. Anyone caught without a valid ticket escapes only with a red face and €40 fine payable on the spot.

➡ Night buses take over the remaining hours, running roughly every 30 minutes.

➡ MetroBuses, designated M19, M41 etc, operate 24/7.

➡ Buses 100 and 200 follow routes linking major sights (see p170).

➡ For information, see www.bvg.de.

Tram

☑ **Best for**... Covering neighbourhoods not served by other transport.

➡ Trams only operate in the eastern districts.

➡ Trams, designated M1, M2 etc, run 24/7.

Bicycle

☑ **Best for**... Exploring local neighbourhoods.

➡ Many hostels and hotels have bikes for guest use, often for free or a nominal fee.

➡ Rental stations are plentiful. These range from convenience stores to clothing boutiques to gas stations to bike shops and bike ranks. Keep an eye out for 'Rent-A-Bike' signs or consult www.adfc-berlin .de (link to Service, then ADFC Branchenbuch, then Fahrradverleih) for addresses.

➡ The website www.bb bike.de is a handy route planner.

➡ Bicycles may be taken aboard designated U-Bahn and S-Bahn carriages (usually the first and last ones), but you need to get a separate ticket called a *Fahrradkarte* (bicycle ticket, €1.50).

➡ For bicycle tours, see p170.

Taxi

☑ **Best for**... Late night and groups sharing the cost.

➡ Flag down a cab, pick one up at a rank or book one on ☎ 443 322 or ☎ 210 202.

➡ Flag fall is €3.20, then it's €1.65 per kilometre for the first 7km and €1.28 for each kilometre thereafter. Rates were expected to increase in 2012.

➡ The short-trip rate (*Kurzstrecke*) entitles you to ride for 2km but only if you flag down a moving taxi and request this rate before the driver has activated the regular metre.

➡ Tip about 10%.

Late-Night & Sunday Shopping

➡ One handy feature of Berlin culture is the *Spätkauf* (*Späti* in local vernacular), which are small neighbourhood stores stocked with the basics and open from early evening until 2am or later. They're especially prevalent in areas with busy streetlife or nightlife.

➡ Some supermarkets (especially select branches of the Kaiser's chain) stay open until midnight; a few even through the night.

➡ Shops and supermarkets in major train stations (Hauptbahnhof, Ostbahnhof, Friedrichstrasse) are open late and on Sundays.

➡ Petrol stations also stock some supplies, usually at premium prices.

Essential Information

....

Business Hours

Top Tip Many boutiques and smaller shops don't open until noon and close at 6pm or 7pm.

Exceptions to the following standard hours are noted in reviews:

Bars from 6pm

Clubs from 11pm or midnight

Restaurants 11am-30pm

Shops 10am-8pm Mon-Sat

Discount Cards

Top Tip An unbeatable deal for culture vultures, the Berlin Museum Pass buys admission to the permanent exhibits of about 70 museums on three consecutive opening days. It sells for €19 (concession €9.50) at Berlin tourist offices (€80) and participating museums.

Berlin WelcomeCard entitles you to unlimited public transport and up to 50% discount to 200 sights, attractions and tours for periods of two, three and five days. Cards start at €17 for 48 hours

and are available online at www.visitberlin.de or at Berlin tourist offices, U-Bahn and S-Bahn ticket vending machines, BVG offices and many hotels.

➜ **CityTourCard** (www .citytourcard.de) Works on the same scheme as the Berlin WelcomeCard and starts at €16. Buy it at U-Bahn and S-Bahn vending machines, BVG and S-Bahn offices.

Electricity

230V/50Hz

Emergency

Ambulance ☏110

Fire Department ☏112

Police ☏110

Money

☑ **Top Tip** The easiest way to obtain cash is from ATMs linked to international networks like Cirrus, Plus and Maestro. Check with your bank for fees and daily withdrawal limits.

➜ The German currency is the euro (€), divided into 100 cents.

➜ Cash is king in Berlin where credit cards are not as widely used as in other countries. Always enquire first.

➜ Report lost or stolen cards at ☏116 116.

Public Holidays

Neujahrstag (New Year's Day) 1 January

Ostern (Easter; Good Friday, Easter Sunday and Easter Monday) late March/April

Christi Himmelfahrt (Ascension Day) 40 days after Easter

Maifeiertag (May Day) 1 May

Pfingsten (Whit/ Pentecost Sunday and Monday) May/June

Tag der Deutschen Einheit (Unification Day) 3 October

Weihnachten (Christmas Day, Boxing Day) 25–26 December

Telephone

➡ Most public payphones work with phonecards, which are sold at convenience stores, post offices and tourist offices.

➡ Berlin's city code is ☎030; Germany's country code is ☎49.

➡ Mobile (cell) phones operate on GSM900/1800. If your home country uses a different standard, you'll need a multiband GSM phone while in Germany.

➡ Buying a prepaid local SIM card (eg at Netto, Lidl or Aldi supermarkets) may bring costs down.

Tipping

➡ Restaurant bills almost always include *Bedienung* (service charge) but most people add 5% or 10% unless service was truly abhorrent.

➡ At hotels, porters get €1 or €2 per bag; it's also nice to leave some cash for the room cleaners.

➡ Tip bartenders about 5% and taxi drivers about 10%.

Toilets

☑ **Top Tip** Guys can have a quaint pee in the octagonal Christmas-tree-green *pissoirs* that are vestiges from the 19th century when indoor plumbing was not yet commonplace.

➡ Free-standing public pay toilets are scat-tered throughout centra Berlin.

➡ Toilets in malls, department stores, public venues, cafe and restaurant are often attended by cleaners who either request a small fe (usually €0.50) or expe a small tip.

Tourist Informatic

The local tourist board **Visit Berlin** (www.visit berlin.de), operates three walk-in offices (listed following) and a **call centre** (☎250 025; ⊙9am-7pm Mon-Fri, 10am-6pm Sat, 10am-2pm Sun) whose multilingua staff field general ques tions and make hotel and ticket bookings. From April to October extended hours may apply.

Dos & Don'ts

➡ Do say *'Guten Tag'* when entering a business.

➡ Do state your last name at the start of a phone call.

➡ Do bring a small gift or flowers when invited to a meal.

➡ Do bag your own groceries in supermarkets. And quickly!

➡ Don't be late for meetings and dinner invitations.

➡ Don't talk about WWII with a victor's mentality.

➡ Don't assume you can pay by credit card, especially when eating out.

Brandenburg Gate (Map 30, D3; ◷10am-7pm; U-/S-Bahn Brandenburger Tor) In the south wing.

Hauptbahnhof (◷8am-10pm; U-/S-Bahn Hauptbahnhof) Near the Europaplatz north exit.

Neues Kranzler Eck (Map 24, E2; Kurfürstendamm 2; ◷10am-8pm Mon-Sat, 9.30am-6pm Sun; U-Bahn Kurfürstendamm)

Travellers with Disabilities

→ There are ramps and/or lifts in many public buildings, including train stations, museums, concert halls and cinemas.

→ Most buses and trams are wheelchair-accessible and many U- and S-Bahn stations are equipped with ramps or lifts. Many stations have grooved platforms to assist vision-impaired passengers.

→ For trip-planning assistance, contact the **BVG** (☏194 19; www.bvg.de).

→ For free wheelchair rentals and a breakdown service, call ☏0180 111 4747 for 24-hour assistance.

Visas

→ Most EU nationals need only their national identity card or passport to enter, stay and work in Germany.

→ Citizens of the US, Canada, Australia, New Zealand and Israel are among those who need only a valid passport (no visa) for tourist stays of up to three months.

→ Nationals from other countries must apply for a Schengen visa with the consulate of the country that is your primary destination.

→ For full details, see www.auswaertiges-amt.de or check with a German consulate in your country.

Language

It's easy to pronounce German because almost all sounds are also found in English – just read our pronunciation guides as if they were English and you'll be understood.

In German, word stress falls mostly on the first syllable – in our pronunciation guides the stressed syllable is indicated with italics.

Note that German has polite and informal forms for 'you' (*Sie* and *du* respectively). When addressing people you don't know well, use the polite form. In this language guide, polite forms are used, unless you see (pol/inf) which indicates we've given both options. Also note that (m/f) indicates masculine and feminine forms.

To enhance your trip with a phrasebook, visit **lonelyplanet.com**. Lonely Planet iPhone phrasebooks are available through the Apple App store.

Basics

Hello.
Guten Tag.   goo·ten taak

Goodbye.
Auf   owf
Wiedersehen.   vee·der·zey·en

How are you? (pol/inf)
Wie geht es   vee gayt es
Ihnen/dir?   ee·nen/deer

Fine, thanks.
Danke, gut.   dang·ke goot

Please.
Bitte.   bi·te

Thank you.
Danke.   dang·ke

Excuse me.
Entschuldigung.   ent·shul·di·gung

Sorry.
Entschuldigung.   ent·shul·di·gung

Yes./No.
Ja./Nein.   yah/nain

Do you speak (English)?
Sprechen Sie   shpre·khen zee
Englisch?   eng·lish

I (don't) understand.
Ich verstehe   ikh fer·shtay·e
(nicht).   (nikht)

Eating & Drinking

I'm a vegetarian. (m/f)
Ich bin Vegetarier/ ikh bin ve·ge·tah·ri·er
Vegetarierin.   ve·ge·tah·ri·e·in

Cheers!
Prost!   prawst

That was delicious!
Das war sehr   das vahr zair
lecker!   le·ker

Please bring the bill.
Die Rechnung,   dee rekh·nung
bitte.   bi·te

I'd like ...
Ich möchte ...   ikh merkh·te ...

a coffee	*einen Kaffee*	ai·nen ka·fay
a glass of	*ein Glas*	ain glas
wine	*Wein*	wain
a table	*einen Tisch*	ai·nen tish
for two	*für zwei*	für tsvai
	Personen	per·zaw·nen
two beers	*zwei Bier*	tsvai beer

Shopping

I'd like to buy ...
Ich möchte ...   ikh merkh·te ...
kaufen.   kow·fen

May I look at it?
Können Sie es   ker·nen zee es
mir zeigen?   meer tsai·gen

How much is it?
Wie viel kostet das?   vee feel kos·tet das

That's too expensive.
Das ist zu teuer.   das ist tsoo toy·er

Can you lower the price?
Können Sie mit   ker·nen zee mit
dem Preis   dem prais
heruntergehen?   he·run·ter·gay·en

There's a mistake in the bill.
Da ist ein Fehler in   dah ist ain fay·ler in
der Rechnung.   dair rekh·nung

Emergencies

Help!
Hilfe!   hil·fe

Call a doctor!
Rufen Sie   roo·fen zee
einen Arzt!   ai·nen artst

Call the police!
Rufen Sie   roo·fen zee
die Polizei!   dee po·li·tsai

I'm lost.
Ich habe   ikh hah·be
mich verirrt.   mikh fer·irt

I'm ill.
Ich bin krank.   ikh bin krangk

Where's the toilet?
Wo ist die Toilette?   vo ist dee to·a·le·te

Time & Numbers

What time is it?
Wie spät ist es?   vee shpayt ist es

It's (10) o'clock.
Es ist (zehn) Uhr.   es ist (tsayn) oor

morning	Morgen	mor·gen
afternoon	Nach-mittag	nahkh·mi·tahk
evening	Abend	ah·bent
yesterday	gestern	ges·tern
today	heute	hoy·te
tomorrow	morgen	mor·gen
1	eins	ains
2	zwei	tsvai
3	drei	drai
4	vier	feer
5	fünf	fünf
6	sechs	zeks
7	sieben	zee·ben
8	acht	akht
9	neun	noyn
10	zehn	tsayn
100	hundert	hun·dert
1000	tausend	tow·sent

Transport & Directions

Where's ...?
Wo ist ...?   vaw ist ...

What's the address?
Wie ist die   vee ist dee
Adresse?   a·dre·se

Can you show me (on the map)?
Können Sie es mir   ker·nen zee es meer
(auf der Karte)   (owf dair kar·te)
zeigen?   tsai·gen

I want to go to ...
Ich mochte   ikh merkh·te
nach ... fahren.   nahkh ... fah·ren

What time does it leave?
Wann fährt es ab?   van fairt es ap

What time does it arrive?
Wann kommt   van komt
es an?   es an

Does it stop at ...?
Hält es in ...?   helt es in ...

I want to get off here.
Ich mochte hier   ikh merkh·te heer
aussteigen.   ows·shtai·gen

ndex

Behind the Scenes

Send Us Your Feedback

We love to hear from travellers – your comments help make our books better. We read every word, and we guarantee that your feedback goes straight to the authors. Visit **lonelyplanet.com/contact** to submit your updates and suggestions.

Note: We may edit, reproduce and incorporate your comments in Lonely Planet products such as guidebooks, websites and digital products, so let us know if you don't want your comments reproduced or your name acknowledged. For a copy of our privacy policy visit lonelyplanet.com/privacy.

Our Readers

Many thanks to the travellers who used the last edition and wrote to us with helpful hints, useful advice and interesting anecdotes:

Jeffrey Barron, Victoria Hirst, Sjoerd Joosen, Knud Orsted, Marijke Joannemijn Starke, Tanja

Andrea's Thanks

Many thanks to the league of local friends and colleagues who so generously supplied me with insights and insider tips, with special mention to

Henrik Tidefjärd, Miriam Bers, Nicole Röbel, Frank Engster, Julia Schoon and Ron Wilson. Kudos to the entire LP team responsible for producing such a kick-ass book.

Acknowledgments

Cover photograph: Brandenburg Gate, Berlin, Gunter Grafenhain/4Corners. Many of the images in this guide are available for licensing from Lonely Planet Images: www.lonelyplanet images.com.

This Book

This 3rd edition of *Pocket Berlin* was researched and written by Andrea Schulte-Peevers. The previous two editions were also written by Andrea Schulte-Peevers. This book was commissioned in Lonely Planet's London office, and produced by the following:

Commissioning Editors Anna Tyler, Katie O'Connell

Coordinating Editors Gabrielle Stefanos, Carolyn Bain **Coordinating Cartographer** Jacqueline Nguyen **Coordinating Layout Designer** Adrian Blackburn **Managing Editors** Kirsten Rawlings, Barbara Delissen **Senior Editor** Susan Paterson **Managing Cartographer** Adrian Persoglia **Managing Layout Designer** Jane Hart **Cover Research** Naomi Parker **Internal Image Research**

Aude Vauconsant **Language Content** Annelies Mertens **Thanks to** Janine Eberle, Ryan Evans, Chris Girdler, Liz Heynes, Laura Jane, David Kemp, Gemma McGoldrick, Trent Paton, Piers Pickard, Martine Power, Lachlan Ross, Michael Ruff, Julie Sheridan, Peter Shields, Amanda Sierp, Laura Stansfeld, John Taufa, Gerard Walker, Clifton Wilkinson

Our Writer

Andrea Schulte-Peevers

Andrea has travelled the distance to the moon and back in her visits to some 65 countries and traces her fascination with Berlin's mystique back to her first stay in the summer of 1989, a few months shy of the Wall's collapse. Born and raised in Germany and educated in London and at UCLA, Andrea has written about her native country for two decades. She's authored or contributed to more than 50 Lonely Planet titles, including the first edition of this guide, all editions of the *Berlin* city guide, the *Germany* country guide and *Discover Germany*. After years of living in LA, Andrea could be happier to finally make her home in a lovely Berlin flat.

Published by Lonely Planet Publications Pty Ltd
ABN 36 005 607 983
3rd edition – May 2012
ISBN 978 1 74179 855 5
© Lonely Planet 2012   Photographs © as indicated 2012
10 9 8 7 6 5 4 3
Printed in China